DIARY OF A GRIEF

THE HEART'S SORROWS

The eggs break on the ploughed-up ridgy earth,
The yolks fill the wounded crying furrows –
What will grow from the soul's dry dearth?
What fertility come from the heart's sorrows?

Diary of a Grief

Peter Woods

William Sessions Limited
York, England

ISBN 1 85072 207 2

Printed in 10 on 11 point Plantin Typeface
from Author's Disk
by Sessions of York
The Ebor Press
York, England

Contents

Chapter   *Page*

1   The First Three Months   1

2   The Second Three Months   21

3   The Second Six Months   43

4   The Second Year   80

5   After Two Years   99

Appendices

I   Quotations   103

II   Books   109

III   Hints on Comforting   110

Note: The events related in the following pages actually happened, and refer to real people. However, to preserve confidentiality, all names have been changed, and I am grateful to the editor who carried out this task. I am also grateful to those who read the first draft and encouraged me.

CHAPTER 1

The First Three Months

31 October 1993

QUAKERS WORSHIP IN SILENCE, in the belief that thus is it possible to listen to the promptings of the spirit. A quite extraordinary thing happened to me in my Quaker meeting for worship this morning. It is now a month since I lost Betty, my partner and companion of over 53 years, who died on 1 October. Understandably the grief of this loss and separation has dominated my thoughts and feelings ever since. As usual, Betty's presence was very much 'there' this morning, very vivid. I was once before intensely aware of the presence of someone who had died not many months before, to such an extent that it made me take action I would otherwise not have done. Is the persistent awareness of Betty's presence merely the continuation of long-ingrained habits, of talking to her, of the continuation of familiar patterns? Or is it something more? If it is nothing more than the operation of well-worn brain circuits, why was I so aware of the message of the other dead person, with whom I had no habit of daily communication?

From no apparent stimulus at all, a short sentence suddenly came into my head. 'Hogs are joyful'. What an extraordinary sentence; how absolutely irrelevant and nonsensical! It might just as well have been 'Pigs fly'. The sentence did not particularly come 'from' Betty, it was just suddenly there. But I then recalled that in all the grinding grief of the last four weeks, there was one short moment when I actually experienced joy; it was when I really entered into the truth and the reality of the fact that she no longer had to bear the awful physical pain and suffering which she had endured. 'A merciful release' is such a cliché that it has tended to make me resistant to acknowledging the truth it platitudinates. But this was something different; I recalled in imagination what it was like when one has endured a gnawing, searing pain for hours and then one suddenly realises it is better; and projected myself into Betty feeling like this; and in that I could rejoice for her. That was a small moment of joy, sensed as a feeling, before it became just an intellectual realisation, and the agony

1

of my own devastating loss took over again. But it was like a small pinpoint of light in a night of total darkness.

Presently, I became aware of Betty as in and suffused by a great oval streaming cloud of joy; I think it was pale yellow in colour, like a ball of golden candy-floss. Dismiss this as a fantasy of wish fulfilment if you like – but there it was. There was something else, too, from that awareness: this was an assurance that the pinpoint of joy would grow for me; it would not take away the grief and the loss and the separation, but, if I did not expect too much or too soon, that could also come in time; and this did not have to be incompatible with the grief.

1 November 1993

Habitually nowadays, I find myself spontaneously talking to Betty; I was doing it this morning, towards the end of my 'quiet time' – which I observe for half-an-hour in bed after making my early-morning pot of tea; it is the time I try to use for what I call 'prayer', although orthodox Christians probably would not recognise it as such. This morning an observation came of its own accord in talking to Betty: 'Considering all that was stacked against us, you know we didn't do too badly.'

Anyone seeing the pair of us when we married would have thought that the auspices could not have been better; in fact we thought so ourselves: both with similar religious convictions, both with the zest of youth, both virgins, both with ability, even both with good looks... Yet a number of things were stacked against us. I suppose the most important was the erroneous assumption, held by the majority in our culture at the time and actively taught by the churches, that humankind is naturally monogamous, that pair-bonding for life applied to the human animal, and that anything else was an immoral aberration. This is a cruel half-truth, as Betty and I discovered ten years after we were married. Humankind's natural pattern is neither polygamy, like many animals, nor monogamy like some animals and many birds. It is 'monogamy plus adultery'. In evolutionary terms, this strategy gives the woman the advantage of capturing good genes to mix with hers *and* male help with the feeding of her children, and it gives the man's genes a better chance of perpetuating themselves than in pure monogamy. The price paid for this successful reproductive arrangement is the pain of jealousy.

That was the first great thing stacked against us when we promised in the marriage service to 'forsake all other, keeping only to each other'. Other things stacked against us were the deep hidden wells of anger in me, and the deep self-doubt and lack of self-confidence in Betty; in both cases these propensities lurked unseen below their apparent opposites. Another thing that might have been regarded as against us was Betty's health, resulting from the back injury sustained in a riding accident when she was young. Apparently she completely recovered, but the insidious demon of arthritis was waiting to attack later, and in particular to strike at that old injury. In fact, I do not consider that Betty's health was all that much against us, because of the fortitude in her character, and perhaps, I hope, the compassion in mine. Maybe the great thing going *for* us was a gritty determination by both to keep the promises we had made in the marriage service 'to have and to hold, in sickness and in health, for richer for poorer, to love and to cherish till death us do part.' This was a genuine and continually renewed commitment. Of course this was at times in agonising conflict with the 'anti-monogamous' efforts of the 'selfish' genes working away inside us.

19 November 1993

Yesterday afternoon I had one of my worst times yet; an absolute storm of uncontrollable grief. I think it was because I had had three lovely days with our elder son and his family, and it was when I was driving home, a journey I had so often done with Betty during the last twenty years, that it began to hit me; at one point I thought I should have to pull in to the side of the road, because it was dangerous to continue with such blurred vision. By the time I got home I was in a pretty shaky state. Then coming into the flat, with no Betty. It was made worse when I foolishly tried to clear the top shelf of her wardrobe. I did this because our cleaning lady was coming next day and I wanted to suggest that we should move there the permanent storage of towels and sheets; we could then use the airing-cupboard properly, as an airing-cupboard, instead of it being very over-crowded with stored items. I started doing it but then found I had to give up, exclaiming aloud 'I can't, I can't, I can't' and dissolving into a paroxysm of weeping. When writing to people over the last two or three weeks I have found myself saying that there was a large part of me that still could not believe that it had really happened. I could say to myself 'She's gone, she's gone', but I still find it difficult to say, and at this moment to write 'She has gone for ever, and you will never see her again.' And I think what happened yesterday afternoon was a breaking in of reality, a facing, perhaps for the first time in seven weeks, that that is true. I suppose this is all part of the process one has to go through.

Some years ago I learnt, from the experience of others, that anger is a common component of bereavement, and was half surprised when I experienced none at all. I believe a bereaved person's anger is supposed to stem either from a resentment that life should have been so unfair in inflicting such pain, or from a feeling that the person who has died has deserted the one left, and that this was selfish and uncaring. I have not felt either of those angers, certainly not the second, and as for the first I have lived for some time now in the knowledge that life consists of a mixture of joys and sorrows, of disasters and blessings. I have had, and have, my joys and blessings, so why should I have any resentment against my present agony? However, I had a strange dream a few nights ago: I was in an African village getting ready to be shown the way the elders were chosen, and people were gathering for the ceremony. I had propped my brand new bicycle against a tree, just close by where I could see it easily. I looked away for a moment, and when I looked back again the bicycle had gone; I presumed someone had stolen it. I was absolutely furious, mad with rage. In thinking about the dream afterwards I naturally wondered if the theft of the bicycle represented my loss of Betty; but how could the symbolism work? It was only in regaling the dream to a friend three days later that I saw it: Betty's wheel-chair, in which she spent most of her time lately, had two bicycle wheels.

I *was* angry recently, after visiting a friend of Betty's and her husband. I thought it would be nice to look them up, because years ago this friend and Betty had been quite close. They were both living in a Scottish village at the end of the war without their husbands and with two small children each, and used to meet to go for walks together and talk their heads off. On this occasion I was with this friend and her husband for three or four hours, and in all that time they studiously refused to talk about Betty, although I gave them several openings to do so. Nor did they ask how I was. I suppose they are among those people who have not come to terms with death themselves and find a recently bereaved person embarrassing and threatening. I drove back from their house boiling with anger. What a contrast to my dear Quaker friends who are so different, and manage to convey their understanding, love and sympathy but without fuss.

21 November 1993

Soon after Betty died, the whole of the hospital episode became blurred in my memory. So much happened, there were so many hours when nothing happened, that it is hard to remember clearly; one had moved so suddenly from the normal to the unexpected. I suppose I do not want to let the whole thing go. So I have written it all down in detail. More briefly, what happened was as follows.

One Thursday, by arrangement with our G.P., I took Betty to the Rehabilitation Unit of the hospital for her to be fitted with some sort of foot support, because first one foot and then the other 'dropped'. By the time we got to the hospital her legs were useless, and it was a great struggle manoeuvring her in and out of the car and in and out of the wheel chair. When we returned next day for the necessary measurements to be taken, it was much easier, because I took her in the new wheel-chair transporter I had bought. Betty was able to stay in her wheel chair throughout, and she said it was comfortable and did not feel insecure. On the evening before, she had asked me if she could drive herself round the block for one last time in our saloon car, because she always loved driving and it was part of her independence. We had progressively adapted our cars to assist her, with automatic gear-box, then hand-controls, and lastly power steering. That weekend was a bit of a nightmare because Betty had become more helpless; she was a dead weight, and more than I could lift by myself because of my own injured back. On the Monday morning I rang the doctor early, and she was round at the house within a quarter-of-an-hour. After examining Betty, the doctor ordered an ambulance.

In the ambulance I was surprised to see the paramedic give Betty oxygen, for I did not realise how ill she was. She had lost the use of her legs two years before when she had a bout of 'flu, but three weeks in hospital had put her on her feet again. I think I thought it was a repetition of the same pattern. At the hospital I had to answer all the questions of the examining doctors as Betty could not give coherent replies. Eventually she was taken up to a ward. At the end of the morning I went home by taxi, chiefly to see to Betty's little dog, Dancer, but when I got home there was no Dancer and no Dancer's basket – instead a note from our dog-walker who said she had taken Dancer back to her home because she did not know what time I should be back from the hospital; and that she could keep Dancer there as long as I wished.

When I went back to the hospital that afternoon and evening, Betty was lying with her eyes closed; she seemed to be in a lot of pain, and did not know me. When I went in next morning I found they had moved her into a side ward on her own; she seemed to be better, and much more comfortable. When I appeared she said to the nurse 'Oh, I know this one!'. (I think the nurse had been asking her questions to try to ascertain her level of consciousness.) Betty and I had some rather sporadic conversation, usually with Betty's sentences not finished. I am sure that at this point I still did not realise how ill Betty was. I went home for lunch but was rung up from the hospital shortly after, to be told that Betty had had a fit and was unconscious. I went straight back to the hospital and found her indeed unconscious. Her breathing was quite laboured. The doctor explained to me the position as they saw it. I have to record that all the medical staff were quite wonderful; I am convinced that they could not have done more in the way of expert skill and care, but in addition it was all done so humanely, in keeping us all in the picture. All the children were informed by telephone, and came as quickly as they could, as well as a number of the older grandchildren; it was wonderful that they were all within travelling distance. A number of Betty's local friends heard about her illness and came to visit; the hospital staff did not try to exclude anyone, saying there were too many in the room; and I saw no reason to exclude any, since Betty was unaware of what was going on, and there was no question of 'tiring her out'. The hospital chaplain visited, and was helpful without being obtrusive.

Our elder daughter Pauline and the Renal Unit Registrar had happened to meet in a corridor, and I believe had had some conversation about the possible use of dialysis for Betty, with some mention of the question of 'quality of life'. I did not know about all this at the time, and when this Registrar came into Betty's room, along with other doctors, and there was discussion and explanation about her condition and possible treatment, he continued his conversation with Pauline and completely ignored me. After enduring this with mounting anger, I felt inclined to say: 'Speak to me, damn you, after all I am only the patient's husband!' However, I did not say it, but forced him to address me by cutting in on what he was saying. Discussing this incident with Pauline some months later, she said that the Renal Registrar's extraordinary behaviour was because he knew Pauline was a nurse and thought she would understand better than I would. But when you know that your life-time partner is desperately ill and you need above all to understand the medical situation, it does not help to be treated like an idiot and of no consequence.

The senior nurse on duty asked me if I would like to stay in hospital that night, an offer I gratefully accepted. The nurses, as well as looking after Betty, were wonderful in looking after me as well, putting meals in front of me for example; in all I stayed three nights in the hospital. Our elder son very kindly offered to stay the night in hospital with me, as there was a second bed in the room; I declined the offer because I knew I needed to be alone. This proved to be correct, as realisation came upon me that Betty was dying, and I had the need to cry out and make quite a lot of noise.

On the Wednesday a conference was arranged for the end of the afternoon conducted by the consultant in charge of the ward, at which all the other doctors were present, and most, if not all of our children. The consultant explained the situation very clearly and succinctly, without using too much medical jargon: the antibiotics had not been able to control the infection and her own immune system was not working; her kidneys had failed, the platelet level in her blood was wrong and they had not been able to improve it, and her nervous system was affected; he had to confess that they did not know anything further that they could do. 'Does that mean that we now have to let nature take its course?' I asked. After the slightest of hesitations he answered 'Yes'. Pauline asked 'How long does that mean?'. 'Difficult to say' he replied, 'it might be a few hours, it might be a day or two'.

As that meant that Betty was dying, I knew there was one thing that needed to be done. She never regained consciousness enough to take her last Communion, but I knew that, as a catholic, she would have wished to be anointed. So I arranged with the chaplain to do it later that day. Initially he queried whether it was not too soon, but Betty's breathing was so laboured that I said I did not see how she could last the night. (The contribution of an Anglican minister who was present, hearing and watching Betty's laboured breathing, was to say 'Isn't it dreadful!' He intended this as expressing sympathy for me, but it could have been better expressed. It was left to *me* to disagree and to put a different complexion on it: I was comforting him instead of him comforting me! That evening Betty was anointed, very beautifully done by the chaplain, with the family present and one of Betty's catholic friends, and a Quaker I happened to meet in the hospital lobby half-an-hour before.

The Thursday was spent in waiting, with visitors, children and grandchildren coming and going. There were a lot of visitors, and I found I did not resent them at all; nor did I take any trouble to conceal the tears which were often running down my face – what on earth did it matter if people saw them, in the presence of the enormous thing that was happening? At one point, our dear G.P., who had found the time to visit the hospital as a friend, not professionally, mopped my face and eyes with tissues; I would have preferred her not to do this, but it was an expression of her own sympathy and she is such a dear anyway I could not resent it – and again, in the light of what was happening, what could it matter?

Our eldest granddaughter had made the suggestion the day before that we should play some of Betty's favourite music on tape, and brought her cassette player. I was able to tell one of them which were Betty's favourite tapes and where to find them. On the principle that the sense of hearing is said to be the last to go, we took it in turns to talk to her; and each had their alone time with her. That evening Tony was the last of the family to leave, about 11.30, and I stayed on for another hour and a half, just sitting quietly holding Betty's hand. Her breathing was much quieter now and the night staff seemed to have made her more comfortable. It felt as if we were communicating, like a kind of private Quaker meeting. Eventually about 1 o'clock I thought I better go to bed, the nurses promising to call me if necessary.

I was back again in Betty's room at 6.30 the next morning, and her breathing seemed easier but even more shallow. Some time before 8 o'clock she had another episode, I imagine such as that previously described as a fit; I informed a nurse, who said she would call a doctor 'to make her easier'. I continued to sit holding Betty's hand, and her breathing became shallower again; stopped for about ten seconds, followed by a sharp intake of breath and renewed breathing. This pattern was twice repeated; and then no more. It was all incredibly peaceful, and at that moment there was an amazing transformation, after all the preceding struggles. Her head lying on the pillow looked just so peaceful and so *beautiful*. I looked at my watch and it was 8.08; on Friday October 1st. I did not call a nurse, but a doctor came in about five minutes later, to whom I said 'I think she's gone'. The doctor confirmed this. I must confess I was very glad I was alone with Betty when she died; I felt quite calm.

Pauline and Tony arrived about 9 o'clock. I was able to telephone our second son, Richard, who had visited his mother the day before, and he arrived a couple of hours later. Susan, our younger daughter, had already left home when I telephoned, so I had to greet her with the news when she reached the hospital. Much of the rest of the day was occupied in telephoning. Lunch in the hospital canteen; visiting Betty's body when it had been laid out in the hospital chapel of rest. A great friend of Betty's brought an arum lily, which she quietly laid before the altar in the chapel. There seemed a great sense of unreality at this time; I just went through the motions of what it was necessary to do.

Eventually the family dispersed and Tony took me home, and stayed the next two or three nights with me. I can remember nothing about the next 36 hours, although I am sure Tony and I started the process of making arrangements for the funeral. What I do remember is going to my Quaker meeting on the Sunday morning. Although in some ways I did not want to meet people, I knew I very much wanted to go to meeting for worship; and it was not only all right, but in fact a comfort, and Friends could not have done it better. I was glad to be able to share my pain with a group of people for whom I had a great affection, and they were not frightened to do their part in the sharing.

On the Monday I had a note from one of the priests at Betty's church informing me that he was going to conduct the early service on the Tuesday morning as a Requiem Mass for Betty; so I went along. The other priest did the same on the Friday morning, not knowing about Tuesday's Requiem Mass. This put me out slightly, because in the notices I had put in the newspapers, I had said that a Requiem Mass would be arranged later. Why do 'officials' at a death take so much upon themselves without consulting the nearest of kin? It can of course be rationalised as 'saving the bereaved' at a time when making decisions is burdensome. But this may be false psychology, as it denies the bereaved some of the actions necessary to bring home, however painfully, the reality of the death – which to start with seems so unreal. For this reason Jews give little help to a widow in making the funeral arrangements and insist that she does everything herself.

I managed the funeral at the church by being completely unfeeling. My only concern was that the service should be according to Betty's wishes, which she had fortunately written out beforehand, and which the vicar went along with beautifully. I had found a prayer of Betty's, written out in her own hand in one of her service books, which I persuaded him to use. The children and I consulted together and decided *not* to have any address – what address could do justice to Betty? It was a lovely sunny afternoon, and as the family gathered outside the church, in plenty of time as instructed by the undertaker, it seemed natural to greet all those coming, and it was as if I was on a reception line! It was almost like being an actor in a play – doing my stuff.

Pauline took me in her car to the crematorium, closely following the hearse. I felt very little, I was going through a public performance. I was disappointed at how Betty's 'special' priest took the crematorium service – dry, formal and unimaginative. Lots of lovely flowers to look at afterwards, and then the tea at the Quaker meeting house. This was a good idea and enabled me to talk to a lot of people I was quite glad to see – but I was still the actor on stage. After that I was able to drop all responsibility for the show and sleep, or feign sleep, in the back of Susan and her husband's car when they drove me back to stay with them for a couple of nights. On arrival they understood my need for whisky!

25 November 1993

I came across something from Cruse's training manual for counsellors to the effect that 'Grief Work' consists of:

1. Experiencing the reality of the death

2. Feeling the pain

3. Adjusting to life without the deceased

4. Saying goodbye and building a new life.

These seem sensible headings under which to consider the subject of bereavement, although I would have swapped round the order of the first two. In my experience the pain is immediate and excruciating; experiencing the reality of the death comes not so immediately, and has to be worked at. My spontaneous expressions of pain (apart from tears, of which more anon) have been to exclaim aloud a hundred times a day 'Oh darling!', or 'Oh my darling!', sometimes supplemented by 'We had so much together, so much'. Sometimes these almost automatic ejaculations have been no more than murmurs, sometimes, when the pain has been particularly fierce it has been a loud shout of '*Darling!*'. Thank God for the privacy of my flat that makes that possible. The other ·spontaneous exclamation aloud has simply been 'Oh God!', more of a moan than something said.

I have looked again at C.S. Lewis's *A Grief Observed*, and find that much of my experience is different from his. I have not experienced his sensations of fear – the fluttering in the stomach, the yawning, the swallowing – nor do I consider my tears as 'maudlin', as C.S. Lewis considered his to be. The restlessness, yes. That was particularly bad at first, but is a bit better now after two months, as I have tried to tackle the things that needed doing – but there are still some things I cannot settle to. I have not 'occupied myself' just for the sake of being occupied, as some people tell you to; sometimes I have just sat with this great cloud enveloping me. When in that state I sometimes found myself leaning back in the armchair and banging my heels on the ground, just as a spontaneous reaction to how I was feeling. Someone pointed out that this was like the behaviour of a small child in a temper-tantrum. I often find myself suddenly taking a great gulp of air, and then blowing it out again; I suppose you might call it sighing. On the first few mornings after Betty died I woke up with a great leaden weight in the pit of my stomach, but that has now gone, to be replaced with a feeling of mere depression. I reckon myself extremely lucky that I have not suffered a great deal of sleeplessness, nor have I had a lot of trouble from my 'irritable bowel' as I well might have done, and the episodes of dysrhythmia and atrial fibrillation have been moderate: I had one of the latter for three hours early on the Wednesday morning in hospital sitting by Betty's bed, and another for a couple of hours on October 20th. What I have found is that grieving is a very tiring business.

I find it hard to take in what anyone says. It is so uninteresting. It seems so irrelevant, compared with this enormous thing which is dominating my mind. It also has the corresponding effect of making me sometimes lose the thread of what I am saying, and ending up in half-sentence, or needing a long pause to collect myself and recollect what it is I am supposed to be expressing.

I do not dread the moments when the house is empty, partly, I think, because there is a sense in which it is still full of Betty; and I need that privacy in order to be able to shout and weep. When I am with people who have known Betty, I *want* them to talk to me and to talk about Betty. I know it hit me badly when I came back into the empty flat last Thursday after staying with Tony, but that was not because there was nobody else there, because there was no 'company', but simply because it underlined the fact of Betty's death and, I suppose, was part of the process of 'experiencing the reality of the death'. Yet I know 'A presence still which makes it a joy to be alone.'

I don't think my tears have been maudlin; in fact I know they have not been. They have flowed spontaneously from the agony; and I knew enough beforehand about bereavement to be aware that you have to let yourself do your grieving, you have to be allowed to mourn, or else it will get back at you later. So I have not felt ashamed of my tears, I know that 'the stiff upper lip' to which I was trained is not in these circumstances a good idea. I do not think I have indulged in self-pity, it has never been anything as self-conscious as that, it has been a spontaneous reaction to pain, like crying out if you scald yourself. What I have been aware of when weeping has been an asking of myself 'Am I over-dramatising all this?' – only to find an answer in the negative. African people know a lot about handling grief and are probably wiser in the way they do it than we northerners; it would never occur to them to ask such a question.

I recognise the temptation to 'misrepresent' Betty. Naturally all the letters I have had saying nice things about her emphasise the writers' particular experiences of her, and two have used the word 'saint'. What they experienced of and from Betty remains true for them. We all have many different facets, and show different ones to different people. Betty was a very complex character, and had many different facets. I suppose I knew more of them than anyone else, but I would not pretend to know them all. She was a very human person, and I prefer to remember her as that, 'warts and all', rather than as a saint; I prefer to remember her as the wonderful partner and companion of over fifty-three years with whom I shared so much, including fun and laughter. In recent years she used to say 'I know I am difficult', as a sort of self-justification for something, or 'I know I am a difficult woman' – until on one occasion I said 'That's nothing to be proud of!'. Not many people knew about the lack of inner self-confidence with which she struggled all her life (thanks to the extent that her mother 'put her down' as a child). Unknown to most people also, and probably connected with that same squashing which she received from her mother, were the torments of jealousy she suffered. For a time I thought she was only jealous over me, until I saw that she was also jealous of her younger sister, and, most violently of all, of Jean S. over the love of her middle years, David M. I have just been talking on the phone to someone in the village whom we have known for forty years and who wrote most warmly of Betty being so kind to her when she lost her husband; whereas another widowed neighbour, whom I thought Betty greatly comforted when she lost her husband, said she found Betty very trying and that she was always getting people to do things for her, in the most charming manipulative way.

Betty and I were two 'intelligent, independent, proud, strong-willed people', sometimes at odds with each other but for long periods finding contentment together. When my retirement from the overseas university in which I was working was looming over the horizon, I knew, as a result of experiencing it on my annual leave, that I could not permanently manage a *ménage à trois* with David M. living under my roof. Fortunately for me, as things turned out, that was a situation I did not have to face. I realise now, as never before, how much pain David's death must have caused Betty – and she could not talk to me about it and I could give her no comfort. But later we were able to acknowledge how glad we both were to have been granted those seventeen years together after my retirement from overseas, when we were able to grow an increasingly precious companionship we had not known in the immediately preceding years.

I should write down something which I don't think I recorded at the time – understandably, because I had not started writing this diary then. It concerns the first ten days after Betty died, and a change which took place after that. In that first ten days, in my acute awareness of Betty, I sensed from her a great anxiety on my behalf, a great anxiety whether I was going to be 'all right'. After ten days this changed, and she seemed quite suddenly reassured, and satisfied that I should be 'all right'. Maybe this was for me an expression that I knew that, current feelings to the contrary, I should be able to survive this disaster.

5 December 1993

I find myself using all kinds of similes and metaphors to express 'what it's like' at the present time – such as being amputated, or split in half. Another occurred to me today, expressed as follows:

> I feel like a burst pipe no plumber can mend,
> No one can turn off the supply from the main;
> I wonder whether this emotional draining will ever end,
> Whether there is ever a lessening of all this pain
> Or a slowing the supply of grief the minutes send
> Or whether it goes on for ever – to make the meaning plain

So many of Betty's things – 'the pathetic detritus everyone collects' – to be 'dealt with', or just left? So many 'little booby traps for the heart'. Going through Betty's wallet gave me a funny feeling, because it seemed like prying, but I think it had to be done; the only alternative would have been to throw the whole thing away unexamined, and that might have meant failing to carry out some wish. It meant that I was able to carry out what I am certain would have been her wish, that certain things, precious to her during her lifetime and therefore preserved, but potentially distressing if fallen into the wrong hands, should be destroyed after she had died. I felt I was carrying out a last trust for her. There were other bits of paper that were an indication of our relationship: two of them, in my handwriting, were poems I had given her but had quite forgotten about

and are indicative, not of a continually 'stormy and contentious' relationship, but that we did indeed have our difficulties but always 'fought
back' to come closer together again. Betty was good at that, and always
insisted on the need for us to have uninterrupted time together, away from
work and house and garden, to talk or just be together. Is it any wonder
that one of my frequent exclamations is 'Oh my love, we've had so much,
so much together'.

THE LAKE

I love this place –
Manmade, I know,
Yet, sun or snow,
It has much grace.

Place undramatic
It soothes and heals,
Gently repeals
A past traumatic.

For some, mere pond
To sail or fish;
For us, a wish fulfilled,
With more beyond.

For us, great gain,
For here the we,
The you and me,
Were born again.

THE FOUNTAIN

I think we have come through –
I think we have crossed the desert;
I think we have found again
The fountain of me and you.

We may have found a new land
Yet still we have to possess it
And see that never again
The fountain gets choked with sand.

In her book *Secret Flowers* Mary Jones comments: 'I was more surprised to find how sexual is death. I now understand how a person whose
partner is dying might, in some circumstances, go out and couple
violently and casually.' Surprisingly, I also discovered how sexual death
is. Not that I had any desire while Betty was dying to 'go out and couple
violently and casually', nor afterwards; nor am I now 'sex-starved' in the
usual sense, because for a long time Betty's poor body had been unable
to sustain making love. But what did disturb me in the weeks following
her death was to find so desperately clamant the rather unusual form of
sexual desire which has plagued me all my life and which Betty, bless her,
was able to provide for. I felt I should not be thinking about such things,
it was Betty's death which was dominating my thoughts. However, eventually I accepted that that was how I was and tried to be honest about it.
I did not 'go out and couple violently', but I did acknowledge my desires
in this peculiar form and satisfied them. Initially I felt bad about it, but
Betty was there, in loving understanding as she had been in life, and that
made it all right. I fully understand Mary Jones's remark on the sexuality
of death.

This sense of Betty's presence is something I do not understand and
find difficult to describe or write about. Is it just my imagination, or is it
something more? In one sense it is there all the time, but there are also
times when it is much stronger than at others. Last week I had a long
discussion with a Quaker friend about the old issue of whether Quakers
were Christians or not. What did that mean? How was the Society of
Friends tackling the issue of unity in diversity? As always, we had good
discussion, really worrying away at the topic, but the remarkable thing
was that I was suddenly aware of Betty's presence (we had not talked about
her) and as the discussion progressed, so this feeling became stronger and
stronger.

One of the things I'm finding a bit difficult is to know what is the
appropriate reply when kind people say 'How are you?'. The trouble is
that this is usually a double question: translated, it means both 'I'm so
sorry your wife died; how are you managing your housekeeping and
domestic things without her, are you feeding yourself properly?' as well
as 'I'm so sorry for your bereavement; how are you coping with the grief?'
On any given occasion it may be difficult to know which question is being
asked, and which to answer – or whether it is both. It depends on the
person asking the question. If you think they *want* to keep it on a surface
level I say just 'Fine!', or 'OK', or 'I'm becoming quite a good cook', or
'I'm well looked after' and explain about the children, about my wonderful Julie who cleans the flat for me and will do anything else I ask her,
and about Dorothy, who does me precooked meals. If I think they *want*
an honest answer to the second question, the answers may be 'Well, I

hardly know myself', or 'Up and down', 'I still feel amputated' or 'cut in half', or 'I feel like a burst pipe no one can mend'. What should one answer?

One difficulty I am having is that I know it is good to acknowledge one's grief and let it flow, usually in the form of tears, yet there is a thin line between that and actually massaging one's grief, in a kind of emotional masturbation. For weeks I have been trying to 'get back' to music, and found something preventing me. I do not know whether this has anything to do with the fact that during Betty's last three days in hospital we played her favourite music for her, or whether it has to do with the fact that she used to play a lot of music at home. When we moved from our former large house to this place, I greatly benefited, because it is sufficiently small that when she had her cassette-player on, or Radio 3, I also got the benefit if I wanted to, although she often used to ask me if it was too loud and disturbing me; usually it was the other way round and I would ask her to turn it up. I have looked at the cassette-player with a view to using it and then become almost 'frozen'. More recently I have had my finger poised on the 'Play' button, and then been unable to press it. Only this morning, after playing part of Rutter's Requiem, I had to go and switch it off because I could not take any more. When I said something about this to a friend, she said 'That was because you were not ready for it.' I have wanted to get back to music because I know how comforting and healing music can be, it can get to emotional spots nothing else can, and yet if I know that a certain piece of music, however expressive for me, is likely to result in tears, is this sensible recognition of my present needs or is it self indulgence? This is one of the many things that is so confusing about my present state – because I have never been here before.

9 December 1993

I did not feel able to have Dancer back until a fortnight after Betty died, and she stayed on with Louisa. When she did come back, I expected her to be unsettled and go looking for Betty, but she showed no signs of doing that. I think it may have been because she had had a break of about three weeks from this house anyway, and was just pleased to see me and be back in her familiar surroundings. In addition, there was probably little 'Betty-smell' around by that time, since it is by smell more than anything else by which dogs recognise people. Four or five days after she came back, Dancer had had her usual walk with Louisa at 9.30 and was sitting in the hall between Betty's room and mine, where I was sitting typing with the door open; it was about 11.30. Suddenly Dancer lifted up her head and howled, and went on doing so for about a minute and a half; I made no move, did not speak to her or try to stop her or interpose myself in any way, until she had finished. That is something Dancer has never done before; she is not a howler; and she has not done it since. It was uncanny. I was convinced it was in some way connected with Betty.

Why am I writing all this? I do not know. It is a kind of compulsion. Is it an effort to come to terms with reality? It began with the experience I had in Quaker Meeting, which was so extraordinary, so 'outside-of-me', so powerful, I felt I must try to capture it. Then why have I continued this writing from there? No one suggested I should. All I know is, that, having started it, if I think of something that belongs to my experience of losing Betty, I feel restless until I have set it down, or at least made a note of it to do so at a later moment of better opportunity.

How incredibly blessed I am in my children (and grandchildren), all so marvellously loving and supportive and available. I see too, as a sort of legacy from Betty, the blessing I have in being in this wonderful flat, because I should never have come here on my own; it was Betty and her needs which almost literally carried me here, and I can just stay on, in what is so perfect for me, with this wonderful sunshine view, out of the patio window doors of the sitting-room, over the fields, not another building in sight, yet all the shops and everything needful conveniently to hand within less than a quarter-of-a-mile in the other direction.

I have already spoken of how there is a part of me that finds it so hard to believe that Betty really has died. My brain and intellect say one thing, my emotions another. There is this extraordinary suspension of belief. I suppose the heart cannot bear to believe it.

This experience has changed my ideas about the helpfulness of letters: letters do help. Formerly I questioned how mere words could possibly be of any use in such a catastrophic situation. But they can. Especially if they talk about Betty, reminisce about her, express appreciatively the writer's knowledge and experience of her. In fact, if people write to me who knew Betty well and they do not do that, I feel cheated. It has been quite extra-ordinary how some of those I expected and wanted to do that, failed to do so, while others were able to do so quite unexpectedly. I have found myself asking whether it was a matter of how much they cared, or of how much literary ability they had. I wanted to collect together all the 'nice bits' written in the letters about Betty, so that to find them I did not have to go through the whole of each and every letter. Accordingly I have gone through them all, selected 'the nice bits', and I am starting to type them out.

I have found myself telling people that I was re-structuring my life, and that I did not want to take on any new things in a hurry. Some people have obviously thought it would be good for me to be busy and have asked me to do things. In fact I find myself very busy indeed at the moment, almost entirely with the consequences of Betty's death (her correspondence, probate and related affairs), and with the kind invitations of friends to meals or drinks, which I do find a help. Admittedly some of the busyness is of my own making, but still consequent on Betty's death – such as writing this, and writing up the extracts about her from all the letters.

A curious thing I have just noticed about myself: rather than talk about 'the time of Betty's death', I prefer to talk about 'when Betty died'. I have consistently tried to make myself unafraid to say that. (I have *never* said 'passed away' or used any of the other ghastly euphemisms.) I don't like the phrase 'Betty's death'. Why is this? Is it because 'when Betty died' is merely a reference to a historical happening, which I don't dispute, whereas 'Betty's death' seems to express an absolute finality which is not how I think of it?

After I had typed out the extracts from the letters, an idea occurred to me that I might use my book-binding hobby to bind them into a book. So this is what I shall be doing in the coming weeks. The following lines 'occurred' this morning:

> O my laughter-mate, where
> Are our laughings together, where?
> Have you left them behind
> Hanging on the air?

23 December 1993

I have been away for a fortnight on an art course for ten days, and then staying for three nights with friends. I have to confess that coming back to the empty house this time was less heart-searing than a month ago when I came back from Tony's. I notice I write 'I have to confess', as if I were ashamed of it being less distressing this time, or as if I did not want it to happen. As already noted, this is a familiar pattern.

> The losing my partner and companion
> Makes me cry out
> For easement of the pain –
> Yet in the same breath I shout
> I never want to be without
> This pain again.

While away I jotted down one or two things on different dates, but they must go down now rather disjointedly. On 18th I noted that it was 11 weeks since Betty died, and I found that I was less often finding it necessary to shout out aloud, or to hit myself or some object. Mind you, as far as shouting was concerned, I had precious little chance, being always surrounded. But on the day I left and went for a walk on Kinder Scout and had miles of countryside to myself, I made up for the previous lack of opportunity! I groan a bit still, but I think the acute, intense pain of amputation is changing to the dull throbbing ache which comes later. I wake up feeling terribly depressed, and wonder whether I would not really rather prefer the sharp pain, and regret its dulling.

I notice both a similarity and a difference from the real grief I knew, the grief of separation from loved ones, each time I returned to my overseas university after leave; that particular grief had some of the same features as my present grief; but the great difference from those griefs is that the separations then were for nine months only; none of them had written into them 'for the rest of your life' like this one has.

On the art course there was a woman in her forties who had suddenly lost her husband only ten days before; it was very courageous of her to come, although at the end she said that in fact it had helped quite a lot. I ascertained at once that she welcomed talking about her loss rather than the opposite, and we did share experiences a bit. In a book she had I encountered a quotation from Rabindranath Tagore:

'Let me not forget for a moment, let me carry the pangs of this sorrow in my dreams and in my wakeful hours.'

From what I have said above it can be seen how much I share that feeling, and with Tagore's authority for it I do not have to think it morbid!

Agnes Whittaker has put together a wonderful anthology on bereavement, *All in the end is harvest* (a quotation from Edith Sitwell). One of the best quotations in it is from Penelope Lively, whose descriptive ability so often gets things just right. 'Loss clamped her every morning as she awoke; it roared in her ears when people talked to her so that she did not hear what they said'; 'it interrupted her when she spoke, so that she faltered in mid-sentence, lost track'. Those extracts describe so exactly how it has been for me. She speaks also of 'the instability of grief', and 'playing games with time and reality', time becoming 'formless, mercurial and unreliable.' Just how it is. A poem by W.W. Gibson speaks of 'the heartbreak at the heart of things'. Just how it is: the beauty makes the pathos all the greater. The depths of feeling that loveliness has touched in the past are now pierced with all the greater poignancy because the feelings are raw and unprotected and aching with pain already.

I find that I get most satisfaction from those writings which well express and describe this grief of bereavement, not those which claim to offer comfort.

26 December 1993

Judy Tatelbaum says that healthy grief, dramatic and even traumatic as it may be, is a three-stage process. First it is fully experiencing and expressing all the emotions and reaction to the loss. Second, it is completing and letting go of your attachment both to the deceased and to sorrow. Third it is recovering and reinvesting anew in one's own life. She goes on to say that it is unhealthy to miss out on any of these stages. When I read of the necessity of 'letting go of your attachment both to the deceased and to sorrow' I found myself shouting through tears 'But I don't want to, I don't *want* to, I don't want to do that.' Does this mean that I haven't yet embarked on stage 2? I think I am already beginning on stage 3.

In the last forty-eight hours I have encountered three people who did not know about Betty's death and had to be told. The first was a local Quaker, not in my own Meeting, for whom I was a 'Visitor' when she applied for membership some years ago, who hailed me as I was walking along the High Street. It seemed quite natural to tell her the news at once, and she did very well with it. The second was a friend and former colleague, and it occurred on the telephone, which made it more diffi-cult; she had visited us less than a couple of months before Betty died. She was really taken aback, and her sorrow and sympathy were immedi-ately apparent, even down the telephone, which is not the best medium for this kind of encounter. The third was when I was having lunch with my brother Alec at Salford House, his 'Residential Home for the Elderly', where one of the carers, nice Irish Florrie, ran into an awful pitfall when she enquired after Betty; I blame Alec for that situation and not ensuring that she knew – but he is hopeless over Betty's death anyway; since it's happened he's never been able to speak of it. I was so taken aback that I could only blurt 'What do you mean?' which was a silly thing to say and only created an even more embarrassing situation for poor Florrie. Into the ensuing silence I think Alec and I simultaneously dropped the infor-mation that she had died, myself giving the detail that it was last October. I felt cross with Alec for allowing this situation to occur, but maybe he is not to blame and this sort of thing is bound to happen. But I felt so sorry for Florrie. She handled it very well, and came round and kissed me, which was the best possible way of handling the situation.

One subtle adaptation (or not so subtle) I am finding is the change from 'our', which comes automatically to my tongue, to 'my'. To say 'my house', and 'my car', instead of our house and our car, comes with a con-scious jerk in an uncomfortable way. Now I am having to replace my habitual 'our' with 'my'. It doesn't come easily. It feels even more artifi-cial, and requires conscious effort, to refer to 'my house' instead of 'our house'.

28 December 1993

My resistance continues against the idea that it is necessary to go through the second stage of grieving by letting go of your attachment to the deceased. Did not a Quaker friend use a better word, and a better idea, when she wrote to me as Betty was dying: 'I write thinking and praying about and with all of you as she moves on into what must surely be freedom. It will also, I feel sure, be a repossession. When my mother, died, after some weary months, my sister and I were back from the Nursing Home and we stood looking out of the window and one of us said "We've got her back again!" and the other said "Yes!"'. Repossession – that's more like it, rather than 'letting go of the attachment'.

I also find myself grateful for those descriptions of bereavement when a parent has been lost, but I cannot believe that it can be so knife-painful as losing a partner of 53 years.

Some of those who have written of their experience of bereavement have spoken of the need to fill up all their time, to keep occupied. Not like that for me; I don't have to fill up all my hours, maybe I'm lucky that they are filled for me. Rather, it is the other way round; I find I need to seek quiet, to be still, to stay gently with this great grief, as a respite and oasis from all this activity. You could say, of course, that I have given myself a lot of occupation by deciding to do the bound version of the collection of extracts from letters about Betty, but in no way was this a conscious 'filling up of the hours'. Nevertheless, it is an activity closely connected with Betty and is probably a good thing to do as part of the process of working through my grieving.

CHAPTER 2

The Second Three Months

1 January 1994

THREE MONTHS SINCE BETTY died. Things are changing a bit, although in some ways they never will, and I never want them to. But I think the visitations of acute pain are a little less frequent now, and instead there is a ghastly depression the moment I wake in the morning. This morning I found it quite difficult to get up; and even after I had got my legs over the side of the bed I sat on it for some time in complete lassitude until I forced myself to go and have a bath. Before that, in the course of a weep in bed before I got up, Betty's voice said to me: 'But remember the blessings', to which I replied: 'Oh, my love, yes, yes, yes, I do, but can they alleviate the pain? The blessings are there all right, and I am deeply grateful for them, but they seem separate from the hurt: both exist, side by side, almost without interacting.'

For the first time, two or three days ago, I did have a moment of happiness, and I had to acknowledge this to myself; and it had to be presented to Betty, for her to be glad of it for me, in place of my feeling it to be a kind of disloyalty. I had got a new photo album and began sorting out the photos of our last years together. It felt in some way connected with making up the book of extracts about Betty. In such simple things can real pleasure lie. That brief moment of happiness made me believe that a more general happiness might be possible later on, instead of this over-all depression beneath the never-moving cloud; perhaps there will be more such moments. At any rate I'm prepared to believe it is possible.

So many people, and writers, give the advice 'Keep busy, keep yourself occupied'. I think I would find it difficult to do that, to do time-occupying things just to kill time, busy-ness for busy-ness's sake, it would seem so pointless. Why bestir yourself when you don't feel inclined to, and when you are feeling so exhausted anyway?. This is where I am so lucky. The book which I am editing connected with my professional work, and various Quaker affairs, are things I was committed to before Betty died; I can't just chuck in the sponge and let lots of other people down, however much one may sometimes feel inclined to; as a friend has put it: 'You don't scuttle'. Editing the book seems a mammoth task, and seems unending. So those things provide busy-ness and occupation with their own fly-wheel from the past. But the other things that are providing me with busy-ness are connected with Betty, so they are to do with and arise out of the great dominating thought and don't need a great push of external energy; I'm referring to all the probate work and all the letters required following the Grant of Probate; and to working on the book of extracts about Betty. So all these things are, in fact, a very good way of 'working at one's grief'.

Writing this screed, is also, of course, another way of 'working at one's grief'. I asked myself the other day how I came to get started on it, because I could not remember. But then, of course, I did remember when I read the first page – it was simply a desire to record the experience I had in that Quaker Meeting, because it was so vivid I wanted to capture it and not lose it. I never foresaw that it would result in writing all this!

I have become more aware in the last few days of what a physical thing grief is: one tends to think of it as a matter of the heart and mind, but it is very much a thing of the body too; it is like an illness, or at any rate a sickness. I also referred earlier to Mary Jones's surprise that death was so sexual. At this juncture I am reminded of the thing that I knew already, that 'sexual desire' is not a matter of the body only but is also a quest for the alleviation of loneliness. Masturbation can be physically very plea-surable, but scores zero for the alleviation of loneliness; that is why it is never completely satisfying. At the present time I find myself having more sexual thoughts than formerly – but that's not surprising, is it, if I am looking for an alleviation of the state of living on my own, when I was not doing so before. It is in no way anything to do with what is usually meant by being 'sexually deprived' or suffering from 'sexual starvation', because it had not been possible to make love with Betty for very many years. I find myself scrutinising women in their summer dresses and trying to determine whether they are wearing a bra or not; I look at couples I meet and try to imagine them in bed; I may even fantasise about being in the woman's bed myself. The New Testament says that that is as bad as actually going to bed with them; I'm sorry, but in honesty I have to report that that is how it is with me; I cannot stop the thoughts coming into my head. What matters is what I do with them; and in actual fact I think that that is what the New Testament means.

3 January 1994

A neighbour who might be described as 'an experienced widow', having lost her husband eight years ago, recently returned from a holiday in Ireland; she said she 'got away' as much as she could because she found this helped, and recommended me to do the same; as have a number of others. They cannot understand why I haven't taken the opportunity to visit Pauline in America. But I have come to the conclusion that everybody's grief is different. The reading I have done has been very helpful in describing a lot of feelings and reactions which I have shared – but I have not experienced them all or in the same order. So it is very useful to have the accounts of those who have been able to describe and write down their experiences in bereavement, but each person's grief is that person's own. It is easy to see that the grief of children for the same lost parent is not likely to be identical. How much more individual will be the grief for the loss of a partner – when no two partnerships are identical.

My granddaughter Chris called in for tea with her boy-friend Jimmy. After tea she excused herself to go to the loo, leaving me to go on chatting to Jimmy on the patio seat; when she had been away ages I began to wonder if she was all right; but I realised subsequently that she had been spending time in Betty's room. When she eventually came back she said 'I'm missing Grandmummy so' and burst into tears; Jimmy and I did what we could to comfort her by holding her hand and putting an arm around her, but I encouraged rather than discouraged her tears. I could not help one reaction passing through me: 'God, if you're missing her, what do you think I feel?' She said she hadn't got to know Betty as she now wished she had done, that there were still things she wanted to talk about. I said 'But you were a bit scared of her, weren't you?' (which is what she had told me a couple of years ago). 'Yes', said Chris, 'but she was a very powerful woman'. 'You're telling me!' came as my almost automatic response – defusing the tension in general laughter.

There continue to be contrasts between the different ways in which different people react to the situation now. On the one hand, Rosamunde's sympathy came over immediately when I first gave her the shock news on the telephone, and again a few days ago most warmly when I took her some letters to post in Ghana; and on top of that she has posted me a card in which she finds good words to write of Betty. On the other hand, there are two people, supposedly very close to Betty and with whom I was quite friendly, who have made no contact at all during the last twelve weeks; that has a very odd feeling about it; but then both are rather odd people. I suppose they just don't know how to.

8 January 1994

How over-confident can you be? The day after I wrote the above, and about things changing, after lunch I was looking through my books to find one that my brother Alec had asked to borrow. I came across one which Betty had given me in 1982, with the fly-leaf inscription in her handwriting. It just made me crumple once more – partly, I think, because it had used our pet names for each other. Anyway, I could only lie on the bed and let the crumple take its course, which was pretty violent; I had to delay going to see Alec for a long time. Crumple returned as soon as I came home again, and it persisted off and on for the rest of the day – until I finally cried myself to sleep.

I have been reading again the extracts from letters about Betty, and I came across the bits about 're-possession'; they make a very good thought: that I have not lost Betty permanently, but I have lost her as I knew her and had her; but that now I can begin a process of re-possession. In fact I think I have been doing that; I exclaim to her so often, that I now have the Betty that I exclaim to; which I know is not the Betty that I had during her lifetime – although I tried not to be possessive in the 'having and holding', which is what we undertook when we married. I suppose I am, as it were, entering into a new relationship with Betty – and that could be regarded as a 'repossession'. Intimately connected to the old relationship – but essentially a new one.

Remembered places along roads we drove together seem to have a particular capacity to hit me all of a heap – one of the categories of 'emotional booby-traps'. Richard called in today, and we went and had lunch at the Three Horse Shoes, which was lovely. We took both cars as he needed to leave straight after lunch. Driving on my own back home I passed a spot which remains vividly in my mind, as it was there early in 1946, one grey winter's afternoon I remember, that Betty and I stopped in our second-hand Austin Seven [why did I initially type 'Austin Heaven?' Let Freud interpret!] to have a picnic tea. We had Pauline and Phyllis with us, aged four and two, and we picnicked in the car because the weather was not warm enough outside. One of the million shared occasions in the course of our long partnership; Betty must have just been beginning to be pregnant with Tony. Well, it all came flooding back and I just couldn't wait for the privacy of my own home to fling myself on a bed and let my feelings flow uncontrollably. All the people whom I believe to be wise say it is good not to try to control the tears when they want to come; usually I have the requisite privacy; although they also say it is sometimes helpful to both parties to share the tears. I think that was so in the early days but not now. When Chris was weeping here the other day and I had my arm round her, my eyes were wet but I was not really weeping. When crying comes upon me now it is pretty violent and I don't think I can do that except in privacy. All the way on the drive home today I was saying aloud again and again 'Oh my love, we had so much together, so much, so much, so much, so *much*'. Later, when I was home, I reflected on how true that was, and that if we had not had so much together the pain would not be so bad now; if we had not had all that together, the present loss would not be so excruciatingly grievous. Put that the other way round: your grief now would not be so great if you had not had all that together. So the logic of that is, as I am grateful for all that we did have together, I should in a perverse sort of way be grateful that my present grief is so great. I can live with that. But it seems I still need a good cry once a week! It's not that I think that I now have to *pay* with pain for all that I had with Betty, I don't believe in the necessity for that sort of balance sheet, to make things fair. Life is not fair, anyway; why should I have had so many blessings in my life, compared with millions of other people? I have been one of the lucky ones, in spite of the present grief. No, I don't believe 'You have to pay for all your pleasures'. I think what I am trying to say is that I should *remember*, when the pain is bad, that the reason for it being so bad is because I had so much that was good with Betty; and that the pain should therefore be the occasion for a wry sort of gratitude.

What, incidentally, *is* pain of this sort? I can understand physical pain: our bodies are provided with sensitive nerves to give us warnings of danger; we should burn ourselves much more often if we did not feel the pain of excessive heat. What sort of nerves are our psyches provided with? And what is their function? What is crying? And what makes us do it?

13 January 1994

It seems that a lot of people work on the grief of their bereavement by writing about it, so I'm not all that peculiar in this. In writing about Betty I am well aware of the danger of beatifying the dead, and I do not want to do that, it is the real Betty that I want to 're-possess'. I know also that there is a real danger of beatification as a result of my typing out all the nice bits out of the letters I received. I know it gives a one-sided picture (which is not to deny the truth of what those bits say). I know that she was not the saint that one or two have called her. Yet I find it difficult to write the negative things – to recall when she has seemed selfish and domineering, manipulating and self-deceiving, when we had rows, when I have said to myself about her 'You bitch!'. There! I've said the negative things because it only seemed honest to do so, although I did not want to. This is all very confusing, because while I have to admit the truth of these things, they were not the important parts; the important parts were fifty-three years of partnership and companionship – dare I even say 'love' – that over-used, misused and misleading word. Admittedly she was such a powerful, wilful and determined woman that, meeting a similar character in me, it was necessary at times for us to put distance between us in order to maintain the partnership and companionship; we both realised this, and sometimes discussed it, in order to preserve what we knew was so valuable between us. The reality of the now is what so frequently comes spontaneously to my lips 'Oh my love, we had so much together, so much, so much', and there is no question about the truth of that; no one knows it quite like I do. Writing this and reflecting on this brings the tears again ... I had not intended it to.

16 January 1994

Iris Murdoch defined prayer as 'paying an attention to God, which is a kind of loving.' Anyway, that is what I try to do for my first waking half-hour, and I light a candle to remind me of what I want to be at. I try to remember those known to me who are in any sort of trouble, and those I love and have a care about. At some point the other morning it suddenly occurred to me that I was not doing this for *myself*. If I could do it for others, and believed it was something worth doing, was I not a bit of an idiot not to do it for myself in *my* grief and depression? By chance this idea was reinforced by someone, who doesn't very often come to Meeting because he joins his wife at the Methodist church, running after me to enquire after me and to say that he remembered me in his prayers every day. Initially that was very humble-making – did I really deserve to be prayed for like that? But it reinforced the idea of praying for myself. The sort of thing that tended to come out was, in semi-anthropomorphic language: 'Lord, I *am* so grateful for all the blessings I know I have and I am very much aware of them – comparatively good health, the osteopath is making my back better, yesterday I was able to walk 11 miles on a day of sunshine and breeze with the country looking glorious in its summer splendour – and that was heavenly ...; the fact that I have such a perfect place to live in and do not have to make any difficult decisions about moving house following Betty's death; that I have the help of someone keeping the house clean and of someone else cooking ready-prepared dishes for me; above all that I have wonderful, wonderful children who are so good to me and that they are all live fairly near. I remember how blessed I am in all these things and I am truly grateful, but Lord I do wake up so full of depression every morning. I suppose I shall just have to put up with it – like a rheumatic joint.' As far as I got any reply it was along the lines: 'Yes, you will have to put up with it, probably for a long time. But remember this: I am in the depression too.' With regard to the children, I think our shared loss has made a bit of a difference in our relationships. We were always pretty close-knit, but I think this common experience has made us more so. My relationship with my children is now different in another respect, because it is now a one-to-one relationship, not a shared one.

I recalled something else, too, which was that I often used to wake up feeling depressed before I was married; marriage banished it. I suppose this depression is a manifestation of loneliness.

Recently I had a very vivid message from Betty. There was something I was contemplating doing, writing something, and Betty begged me not to. I could hear her saying 'Please, *please* don't do that'. I was able to reassure her that I would not. It was she who definitely made me go back for my anti-fibrillation pills after I had initially set out without them on my walk yesterday. It was her voice also which said to me yesterday evening 'There you go, driving yourself again; you know you have no need to now.' Were these messages just my memories of Betty and my imagination, or are they something more? I cannot know, but I am ready to believe they could be 'something more'.

21 January 1994

I think I *am* beginning to be more accepting of the fact of Betty's death. I don't think I ever really screamed to have Betty *back*, I screamed all right (and still do sometimes) but just from sheer pain. For a long time I found it difficult to *believe* that she had died, and yet the idea of her coming back seemed unrealistic. But I think the fact of her death is now beginning to sink in, so I suppose I am beginning to come to terms more with the reality of it.

I have already mentioned my disorientation where time is concerned: Jill Truman has a good phrase for this disorientation in relation to time: 'groping about in a time-fog'. She also refers to the 'compulsion' to write things down – which it is obvious from these pages I have shared.

23 January 1994

I had a second fleeting moment of happiness yesterday. A friend had given me a marrow, and I was preparing a marrow cheese such as Betty used to give me, on the lines of a cauliflower cheese. I had always done the peeling of marrows for Betty, and I found the recipe in her cookery book for cauliflower cheese – and, hey presto! I was *able* to do it. Somehow this gave me a brief moment of happiness; and I know it did the same for Betty.

I find nearly all the people who have written about the loss of their loved one tremendously preoccupied with the present whereabouts of the missing one, their state of being, their state of mind, their well-being or otherwise. I have not found myself so preoccupied. I *know* I cannot know. I *cannot* know. I cannot *know*. That being the case, I am left with my hunches, with my intuition; and with that I have to be content; and I am content. And my hunch tells me that the present Betty (whatever that means) is now full of joy. I know that that may be wishful thinking, product of memory and imagination; OK; but that is nevertheless a very strong hunch.

27 January 1994

I have known Virginia for several years, and once talked to her about the Cruse organisation, the local branch of which she had started and to which she now devotes a great deal of time and energy. I felt sure she could not have heard about Betty's death because on the only occasion I met her she said nothing about it. So when I saw her at a meeting I was attending, I ran after her when the meeting broke up and told her. She said: 'Oh, I'm so sorry. Would you like to come and talk?' So I said yes. Four days ago I had a long talk with her. She not only has had the experience herself of losing her husband, but also she has had a great deal of experience in her work with Cruse. I felt she would have a lot of wise things to say as a result, and in less than two hours we got to know each other as never before. She found the reason for my preferring to speak of 'Betty having died' rather than of 'Betty's death': she pointed out that there was a finality about the latter phrase, an event that had happened, whereas the former spoke of a process – which, in a sense, was still going on. When I said that I had been quite surprised, following what I had learnt and read about bereavement before Betty died, that I had not experienced feelings of anger, she said in a warning voice: 'Not yet!'. Virginia called in question something else: I told her about writing this and how it had become almost a compulsion; I referred to C.S. Lewis's confining himself, when engaged on a similar piece of writing, to four notebooks, and Anne Jones to the life of one type-writer ribbon, but that I had no such self-imposed limit and supposed that I should stop indulging myself in this way after six months. Virginia said 'No! Don't do that. That would be assuming that after six months you should be "better", and you cannot give yourself a time-table like that.'

Two days ago Maureen came to tea. She is a very understanding and empathetic person, with whom I had talked quite a lot about Betty's dying. In fact she herself found Betty's death a considerable personal loss, because they were friends before I got to know Maureen, and they had frequent contacts. I had read her some of the extracts which appealed to me from some of the books about bereavement. Came to the following in Jill Truman's *Letter to My Husband*: 'If I could sleep naked in your arms – any man's arms, perhaps – just sleep, no sex, just feel the comfort of your arms, I could face all the rest on my own.' I was surprised at how immediately Maureen understood that, and even more when I said 'Could you do that for me?' how readily she agreed. It was just that, lying in each other's arms, no hint of sex, no embarrassment, but marvellously comforting. I did not weep, but what came naturally was the need for deep intakes of breath and then letting it all out in one go; I suppose you could call it sighing. It was as if I was releasing onto Maureen some of the stored-up emotions against the showing of which I am involuntarily on guard most of the time, and Maureen in her generosity was helping to carry them for me.

I suppose what I am working towards is *acceptance*. Which doesn't mean a denial of the enormity of the loss. I still feel 'I can't bear it; I hate it; I can't endure it.' I hate the trite cliché 'Life has to go on', because there is the overtone in this of 'Business as usual', 'Back to normal', which emphatically is not the case, and I deny it. But I have to recognise that in fact I *am* bearing it, that I *am* enduring it; that there are moments when this great thing is not totally filling my consciousness; and that these moments are slowly becoming more frequent, and of longer duration. I cannot change this situation, I cannot reverse it, it is something I cannot control. So I can either for evermore be caught up in my loss, my grief, my mourning, or I can say: 'I can't change this situation, so I had better accept it. I don't like it, in fact I hate it, so I might as well come to terms that this is how it is. It is not a case of stoically 'putting up with it'; of grumbling about it but being demonstrably 'brave'; in fact it is emphatically *not* 'resignation'; that is really a negative reaction to the situation, not a positive one. 'Acceptance' is a positive thing. How often Betty used to urge people, including myself, to react positively rather than negatively to their situation.

1 February 1994

Four months since Betty died. I see that a month ago I said I thought things were changing a bit. What I note now is that I think *I* could be beginning to change a bit – and am beginning to be aware that I might do so more in the future. Does this relate to a new idea I have picked up from the book on death by Elisabeth Kübler-Ross which Virginia Ross lent me? This is the idea that bereavement can be a time of *growth*. Theoretically I can see that this could be so, first of all arising out of the intense emotional experience, stimulating/releasing growth, knocking one out of one's hitherto unquestioned and habitual patterns of thought; and secondly as a result of no longer having the influence/constraints of the dead person. Oddly enough Helen said the same thing about growth in bereaved persons when I visited her today; she said she could not speak from first-hand experience but that she had observed it in five or six cases; and she is, I should think, a fairly perspicacious observer.

Helen knew Betty very well and saw her frequently. She told me much more than she did before about Betty knowing she was going to die, and that they had talked about this a lot in the three months before it happened. Helen half apologised for the fact that Betty had been able to talk to her about it but not to me. I said I didn't feel a bit offended or chagrined about this, either with her or with Betty; I could quite understand Betty over this, if she had a presentiment that she was likely to die soon – she would have wanted to protect me, not to 'worry me' with it. But I was astonished at the things Helen now told me, and apparently how clear in her mind Betty had been that it was going to happen soon. She swore Helen to secrecy not to tell me at the time, but gave her permission to do so after it had happened. She said Betty had said she would keep an eye on me for a bit after she died to make sure I was all right. I am rather grateful to Helen for having waited for four months before telling me so specifically and in such detail. I think I can believe her; I don't think Helen was just trying to increase her own importance; but I find the idea that Betty knew she was dying in the weeks before she did is something new again which is taking a bit of getting used to. Helen said she was glad I was writing things down, as that was likely to become of help to other people; she said she had made a whole lot of notes from five years ago when she thought her husband Jack was dying at the time he was having chemotherapy for his cancer, and that she would eventually write this up. She agreed with Virginia about not setting a term to my writing but suggested I might bring it to a point where I could put it into a state where it could be seen by other people, but if I felt inclined to go on writing for myself I might well do so.

Another thought has come to me: yes, it is true that the blessings do not diminish the pain, the pain does not diminish the blessings, they operate on different planes without meeting although both are reality, both are there, and I have to hold both together – *but* what would it be like *without* the blessings? I should be in a real pit. So perhaps the blessings do mean that I am not in quite such a deep pit as I would otherwise be.

17 February 1994

About a fortnight ago I had a visit from a friend who used to know me well, and in a subsequent card she referred to me as a person of sudden mood changes, and that one of these had occurred while she was with me. I was quite unaware of this. However, I have now noticed one such change of mood: I was away for a week in Derbyshire for my second art course and then returned home again for the official opening of the new Village Hall, with which I had been involved. I have been very busy ever since, and have experienced a certain reluctance to getting back to writing these observations – whereas before I went away I was always eager to write and record my feelings. In fact there was almost a compulsion to do so. So here would appear to be a change of mood; I wonder why.

I can record a moment of happiness, on my second day away at the art course, when I was just getting all my things out in preparation for getting down to work. On the other hand, I experienced rage a few days later when, in common with others, I had to pack up all my things again and was expected to work in impossible conditions in my bedroom because the managers of the centre decided to take over the studio for a family party. I felt cheated. I found that tears of rage became tears for Betty .... of which there had not been any for a week or more.

I have spoken several times of the expectation of anger in connection with Betty's death and my not having experienced any such anger. I don't think I mentioned a dream I had about three weeks ago. A frequently recurring dream I have had for years, with many variations and differences of locale and surrounding circumstances, is that I am desperately hunting for somewhere to open my bowels and finding nowhere, or that all the places are occupied, or that there is some other sort of obstruction. A psychotherapist once analysed these dreams as indicating I was full of a deep-seated anger which I was unsuccessfully trying to get rid of (excrement = anger). In this dream three or four weeks ago, I was in this same situation of desperately needing to relieve myself, finding the most enormous lavatory bowl you have ever seen (as big as a large arm-chair!) but unable to use it because it was full of Betty's clothes and disability gear. This I then proceeded to fling out as fast as possible all over the place. Of course an interpretation seems obvious, if you believe in such interpretations: that in fact all that I had done for Betty's disabilities, which I would have said I was doing out of love and compassion (which could also be true at the same time) I nevertheless resented; but I had not allowed myself to admit to this resentment – not how I 'ought' to be feeling at all! Maybe in the dream I was now both acknowledging the resentment and getting rid of it.

An American writer says that in acute grief the element of guilt is always present. 'This is probably due to the ambivalent quality in the love relationship where there is self-giving and self-satisfying at the same time, a craving for mutuality between the lover and the beloved, as well as the resentment at the loss of freedom that love inevitably entails. When the love object dies the feelings are set free and there is guilt.' I am sure there is deep wisdom in that. I think I have tended to repress my guilt feelings in this situation, saying to myself: 'I have no reason to feel guilty'. And yet I know that the niggling feeling has been there – particularly in enjoying my present freedom – e.g. in going to a Shakespeare play at Stratford-on-Avon, which I have never been able to do before. Yet I know how wholeheartedly Betty would approve of such doings, and be glad for me to be able to. Then comes the other pang; I want to be able to tell her all about it – and she is not here to tell. That of course goes for a lot of things: I know there was something the other day which I wanted to share with her, something rather amusing but naughty about some person, and I realised that there was *no one* else I could share it with, it would have had a potential for mischief which with Betty it would not have had.

I have been rather surprised that I have found myself so ready to tell the story of Betty's death to anyone who will lend an ear. In fact I am still doing it, in letters, in reply to late letters of sympathy which I continue to get, from people who have only just heard about her death. I suppose also that that is why, five months later, I am still anxious to have the hospital report; I saw my G.P. about this again two days ago and they are still having difficulty in getting it out of the NHS bureaucracy.

A quotation from Rakoff's "Psychiatric Aspects of Death in America" in *Death in American Experience*: "Mourning is essentially a process of unlearning the expected presence of the deceased." That is a good way of putting it. This unlearning is difficult, and it is painful. It is a common experience that it is harder to unlearn old habits than to learn new ones; the old habit in this case being of fifty-three years duration.

I suppose the acute grief is now settling into depression. This has been worse during this last week, I suppose because I am back in the flat. I find I tend to do things more slowly and lethargically, not my usual brisk self. When my superego says 'Come on, get on with it!', I am apt to reply 'Why? What's the point?' I still exclaim 'Oh, darling' aloud dozens of times a day, but it is in a sad and regretful intonation, not the former vehement one, and I haven't shouted it, or yelled a meaningless sound, as I was doing a couple of months ago. I still occasionally groan aloud. I feel I want to shout 'No!', which presumably represents a continuing difficulty in accepting Betty's death. I suppose I should try to turn this into shouting 'Yes!', although I know this would be followed by a subdued and rather grumbling 'I suppose so'. What a lot of suppositions in this paragraph; here's another: I suppose it indicates a continuing state of confusion.

24 February 1994

Well, last Saturday I did just that, shouted 'No' *and* 'Yes'. I was out walking Dancer between our village and the next, where I can let her off the lead and she can run free; being out of earshot of any houses, I took the opportunity to yell 'No!' at the top of my voice, two or three times; and then dutifully followed it with the 'Yes'.

Contrary to when I last wrote, I find I am again desirous to go on writing this account. I have wondered why, and I think it is that I don't want to lose the bit of Betty that is now.

In this continuing confusion during the last few months, I've always been hazy about the days of the week. Now I'm beginning to get hold of the days of the week better now, although I sometimes have to think very hard where in the week we are, whereas before Betty died I was always very conscious of it. It's a bit like the fact that I always know where South is; if I am in a new run of country and don't know where South is, I am never comfortable until I have got myself oriented. Although I am now better on the days of the week, I'm still no good on the months, and even less on the seasons. There has been no winter for me this year.

Two days ago I had another long talk with Virginia. She is wonderfully easy to talk to, and we ranged over a lot of things. One of the things she mentioned was that although you share the loss with your children, the two losses are two very different things; grown-up children can have no conception of how acute one's own grief is; nor, really, would one want them to. She had quite a lot to say about realising how *normal* I am in having all these extraordinary swirling, paradoxical, ambivalent, contradictory feelings ..... and that those who have not experienced this, *cannot* know how it is. Thinking about this afterwards, I realise that I now divide the world into those who have had this experience and those who have not. Last Saturday I had lunch with an old college friend who is very sympathetic and, as a parson, is also supposed to be trained in pastoral care. I talked quite a bit about Betty and my present situation. At one point I was trying to explain some of my feelings, and I suddenly realised there was no point in going on, because he had not the remotest idea what I was talking about. I now not only divide people into those who have had the bereavement experience and those who have not, but it has also changed my view of the proportion of joy and sorrow in the world, the balance of happiness and suffering: seeing that there are so many people in the world who have had this experience, it makes me realise how universal this load of sorrow is and how much of it there must be in the world; yet also how much of it must lie concealed – because 'life has to go on' and most people outwardly put up an appearance of 'getting over it'.

I have come across a sheet of paper torn out of a notebook with something on it which I wrote two or three months ago.

'It seems to me that death can be compared to a phase-change in physics. Water becomes unrecognisable as such when it turns into ice, although its essential elements are still there; water becomes unrecognisable as such when it turns into steam, although its essential elements are still there. When someone dies, that person becomes unrecognisable as the person they were; yet perhaps the essential elements of that *person* (as a person, apart from their body) remain somewhere, in a form we are not equipped to recognise.'

1 March 1994

Betty's birthday (7.30 p.m.). It has felt very funny today – funny peculiar, of course. I haven't quite known what I feel, or what I am supposed to feel. For the first time today I feel extraordinarily – and I mean 'out of the ordinary' – 'quiet'; in fact, with an unexpected sense of peace.

How blessed I am: Pauline rang me before I was out of bed, Phyllis came and ate her sandwiches with me at lunch-time, Richard then rang and Tony a few moments ago – all so caring and warm. Julie also had not forgotten that it was Betty's birthday. Presently I am going out to supper with Pauline.. It has been good to recall the very happy family celebration we had last year for Betty's 75th birthday. Without my asking her, Julie said something about Betty having spoken in the month before she died that she felt she was not long for this world, confirming what Helen had said. Helen had also said that Betty had told her that she had said something of the same sort to the Vicar. However, when I went to see him last week, the Vicar denied that Betty had said anything like that to him. So what??? I wanted to ask him about this, and about giving something to the Church in memory of Betty. He suggested a pair of silver candlesticks for the altar; he is going to look into prices. Julie also passed on to me something it is nice to know from an independent source, and that was how pleased Betty was four days before she went into hospital that I had bought her flowers. Another happy thing is that I have had the last film in Betty's camera developed and there is a lovely one of her that I took, in which she is sitting in her wheelchair on the path outside the patio here, talking to the pony in the field across the fence.

3 March 1994

Swings of mood, oh yes! Did I say two evenings ago that I felt peaceful? Well, yesterday was terrible, fratchety and depressed to a degree. I got some relief after going to bed when the weeping began, and making quite a lot of noise, and at one point shouting out to Betty. Such is the conditioning of my upbringing and of my culture that I still find it quite difficult to confess this even to the privacy of my word-processor. How lucky I am that I am living alone and can do this sort of thing when it comes upon me, without other people around, and the consequent embarrassment for them and myself. How deprived are the bereaved who do not have this privacy.

Things from the Kübler-Ross book: 'Our choice is not to avoid pain, our choice is only to permit pain to be experienced fast and hard or to be experienced slow and hard; that is our only choice.' I can see that; I did not try to avoid the 'fast and hard' at the beginning, but the 'long and hard' seems to be continuing as well. I suppose it depends what you mean by 'long', and five months should not be counted as 'long'. But how long does it go on? I think it is the not knowing that which helps to make the present stage so full of depression. I suppose I must accept Edith Mize's (also in the K-R book) 'There is no time limit on grief.' The same writer said: 'Grief cannot be hurried, but eventually an emotional balance returns.' I suppose that is my present state; I am emotionally completely off balance – because one emotional feeling dominates all others and tips the balance over to that one side. The same writer says: 'My grief consumes me at times, but I will learn to live with my loss' and goes on to speak of making a conscious effort to smile. I do not have to do that: I have no difficulty in smiling, in cracking jokes, in laughing – but it is only half of me that is doing that. I believe it is right to do that, but sometimes when it is happening I want to scream at the other people present 'Can't you see that that is only half of me, and have you no imagination what it is like in the inside half?'

I am aware, both from reading and from what I know in myself, that what has to come is 'acceptance', and that there is difficulty over this, and a certain amount of inner resistance against it from me. Not intellectual acceptance, of course, that is easy and comes at once; what is totally different is the emotional acceptance. Kübler-Ross says that emotional acceptance takes time and work and pain and hurt. But what *is* 'emotional acceptance?' Do the Nichols (in K-R book) have the answer? 'The ultimate goal of the grief work is to be able to remember without emotional pain and to be able to reinvest emotional surpluses.' I wonder what that last phrase means.

Edith Mize (in the K-R book) says that ambition, goals to achieve, and hope in the future make life worth living. I don't think I've got much left in the way of ambition; my greatest personal hope for the future is to remain healthy till I die; of goals to achieve, oh yes, I've got lots, although for the time being they are mostly pretty short-term – which I think is all right. The most important one for me at present is to complete making the book with the extracts about Betty; and other goals are and have been to clear other things, one by one, out of the way to make time for that. For just that reason it was satisfactory (although terribly boring) to complete going through the manuscript of a monumental book, which the author asked me to do, and which I started over six months ago; it has been hanging over me, in the back of my mind, ever since.

4 March 1994

I have not been able to play any music for about four months – perhaps because we had played Betty's favourite tapes to her when she was dying. I'm not sure, actually, whether that is the reason, but perhaps rather because I instinctively know that music will break down my control. For it does; yesterday I tried Classic FM, and finished up hopelessly weeping; I could not stop. The agony seemed as sharp as ever. It seems unfair (is anything unfair?) that I should now be having the acute pain *and* the depression. It was very heavily on me yesterday, and when I woke up this morning it seemed very tempting just to stay in bed: no one coming to take Dancer for a walk, I could just let her out onto the patio a few times, I could ring the lady I usually take to Meeting and tell her I could not give her a lift, just stay in bed all day ...... I seem to be getting worse, not 'better' – whatever that means; perhaps I have to go down even deeper into this pit before beginning to climb out again. Perhaps there's something in the process one cannot learn any other way. 'Truth lies at the bottom of a well.' Dear Charlotte, my 24-year-old granddaughter, came to visit me yesterday, and she is wonderful; at one point she said 'You need a hug' and climbed into my chair and gave me a prolonged one. In talking about present times, she at one point suggested I must have experienced, or be experiencing, despair; but I was able to say that that was not so. However much agony and depression there might be, I would never call it despair; I knew that basically everything was all right.

I had another encounter with one of those who cannot handle death. This time it was Nat Wigan. I've been thinking for some time that if he wasn't going to make contact with me, I must take the initiative. I was galvanised into doing so by his being joint author of an offprint which Annette sent me, together with the warmest of covering letters. When I got Nat on the phone he asked briskly what he could do for me; said he had heard my news from Annette, had been in my area not long ago but didn't know exactly where I was living now and didn't know whether I would want to see him or prefer to be left alone. He referred to the big 'hole' in my life with which I had been left. I find it quite hurtful, these people who are too embarrassed to do or say anything; and in this case someone who had quite a relationship with Betty. I related Nat's response to Virginia when I saw her again, and she thought it was most extraordinary behaviour. She commented that in the bereavement experience you discover who your friends are; some you find do not know how to be be very good friends in these circumstances; others, whom you had not before thought of as 'real friends', you discover really are. One of the gifts I have received in my present situation has been finding such a friend in Virginia herself.

I spoke to her of the difficulty of achieving emotional acceptance of Betty's death, which made her say something about 're-investment'. The phrase 're-investment in living' in Kübler-Ross was one which I had puzzled over for some time: was I not doing so, getting on with a new life? Yet I did not feel I was really achieving emotional acceptance. Virginia explained that I had invested so much in loving Betty and expressing it in looking after her in daily living, and had received so much in return, but now that was all suddenly gone. However, she suggested I was beginning to invest that love in my children and grandchildren and in new relationships with them, and receiving it too; that was the kind of re-investment meant.

I realise that because this bereavement remains one historical fact, the one dominant thing in my mind all the time, I tend to think of grief as a 'steady state', and then get knocked over by the surprise of a great wave of it suddenly hitting me at an unexpected moment. A picture of myself standing in surf is therefore a better analogy than any steady state. The great waves do break over me at unexpected moments and at random intervals.

Am I doing this writing 'to Betty?' I do not think so. Possibly rather it is to myself – or rather 'for' myself, because I do not want to lose anything. One of the difficulties is being totally honest. Virginia referred to a man who had lost his wife and he had said 'If this experience was not so terribly painful it would be very interesting!' In my case I wonder whether I am writing of this experience because it is unique for me and I know it is important. I don't want to lose anything. Is the reason I do not want to lose anything because it is all part of my experience of Betty, and I do not want to lose any of that?

12 March 1994

I've just come back after being away for six days, first with Richard, and then in Derbyshire, in an attempt to go on a balloon flight, abortive because of high winds. But on my return I discovered one thing which I suppose must be counted as 'progress'. I welcomed coming back to 'my home', not simply to a big hole that was empty of Betty.

On my way down to Richard I called in on Elizabeth Munnings who was in hospital. I found her much worse than the friend she lived with had given me to understand, in fact she seemed to me to be dying, in spite of the fact that I think she did know who I was and it seemed to give her great pleasure, repeating something like the word 'Wonderful'. I called again three days later on my way from Richard's to Derbyshire, and she was much further gone; in fact it seemed so difficult to see how she could last much longer that after leaving the hospital I found my eyes filling with tears all the way to my destination. A close friend of Elizabeth's, who was also at the hospital, exclaimed 'Oh I wish the Lord would let her go'. She was such a dear friend, and from so long ago, before Pauline was born. About six o'clock on Saturday, Phyllis (who was Elizabeth's goddaughter) rang me with the news that Elizabeth had died, at the end apologising for being the bearer of bad news. I said: 'No, Phyllis, it is not bad news, it is good news'. When I went up to my room after that before dinner, I found myself weeping for Elizabeth, which of course became weeping for Betty. After dinner, and the necessity to be sociable and giving my attention to that, I came back to thoughts of Elizabeth and I was in fact filled with gladness that she had been released.

The day before I went away I said something to Virginia indicating that I felt I ought to have made more 'progress' in five months. She said: 'Five months! But that is a very short time in the scale of these things. Don't be so impatient. What is five months after living with Betty for over fifty-three years!' That certainly puts it in perspective. Virginia recounted how in her own case an old lady had said to her: 'One day the clouds will roll away, and the sun will come out.' Virginia said that at the time she did not believe it, but she asserted that it did happen, eventually; even if the clouds came back sometimes.

I knew a moment of joy this morning. I had collected Dancer from the kennels and decided to give her a walk, and suddenly had the bright idea of trying a new walk in the hills near the kennels. It was splendid; not only is it lovely up there anyway, but I was able to let Dancer off the lead and it was a joy to see her racing all over the place; particularly was this so when she used her own special four-footed take-off to leap over the long grass or tufts of big weeds ... (She is lying on my lap while I type this, and she has just made the word-processor squeak by laying her chin on the key-board, so if something strange appears it will be her fault, not mine!)

For a long time I have said that there were no such entities as 'persons' but only 'interpersons'. Listen to this from Mwalimu Imara (whoever he is) on p.150 of the K-R book: '... the threat of losing relationships with other significant persons in our lives is greater than the fear of losing our own life. We are animals who think of ourselves through our transactions with other persons. We are basically social being fellowpersons. And we cannot break our bonds with one another without becoming of no value.'

I have several times expressed my anger at those who won't listen, and my gratitude to those who do. 'Proper' listening is an effort and a gift. Good words on this occur in the K-R book (p.157). 'We seldom think of conversation as commitment, but it is. I find that expressing what I really feel and telling another person what is actually important to me at the moment is difficult. It requires a "commitment" on my part to do so, and I sense that this is true for most of us. It is equally difficult to listen. We are usually so full of our own thoughts and responses that we seldom really listen close enough to one another to grasp the real flavour of what the other person is attempting to convey. Creative communication in depth is what allows us to experience a sense of belonging to others.' How true this all is, and how lucky I am to have a listener like Virginia. The 'commitment to listening' was also very true of Betty, consciously so, even if she did not use that phrase.

Malimu Isara says that in dealing with significant change situations in our lives, we go through a process very much like that of the dying patient, as illustrated in the five stages he lists (denial, anger, bargaining, depression, acceptance). Learning to live life as a dying person is not unlike the relearning necessary after ... a separation from an important person. People are more able to move through the five stages who are willing to converse in depth with significant others about what their present experience is like, meet others on equal terms, that is, are able to enter into real dialogue with others when both can share what is 'real' with the other, and accept the good with the bad.

This month's "Quaker Monthly" had two pieces about bereavement, neither of which I found very good, illustrating once again, I suppose, how different is the experience of different individuals, even if there are recurring patterns. Harold Dennis, in "Grief: mourning or release" says 'I am not the weeping kind', implying that he did not weep; all I can say is 'Poor chap'. Later he said 'The sense of loss seems to be absent'. Seeing that it was of his wife he was speaking who had died only three or four months before, I find this totally impossible to understand. The extracts by Laura Conyngham, who lost her son to leukemia, are more understandable: 'How can I be so "all right" after only seventeen months?' 'Healing is knowing that the tide has turned. Grief waves still crash over me, and always will, but the storm is over.'

24 March 1994

Yesterday was twenty-five weeks since Betty died.

'Grief waves still crash over me, and always will, but the storm is over'. OK for someone after seventeen months – but it doesn't feel as if the storm part is over for me yet. Sometimes I think it may be calming down a bit, and then the gales blow again. To change the metaphor, it's like having a bad sore following a deep abrasion; you think it's healing, and then something knocks the protective scab off, and out pours the blood and pus again ... I find different metaphors like this coming into my head to describe my condition – I suppose it is the subconscious trying to explain and come to terms with what is so confusing and unexperienced-before. The scab on my wound has been knocked off three times this week, and it makes one feel unprotected and vulnerable. As a result I find it difficult to rely on my self-control. This does not matter when I am by myself, but it is difficult when I am with other people.

The first occasion was when Beethoven's Fourth Piano Concerto came up on the radio, and that that should have tipped me over is not surprising, I know how that sort of music can get inside me. The second took me completely by surprise, at the mid-week 'drop-in' Quaker meeting: I had had a very 'scratchy' forty-eight hours and I had been spending the time in Meeting laying all the stupid irritations and disappointments at the feet of the Eternal. In addition, I had two greater causes of unhappiness – my continuing depression (over the loss of Betty), and last Sunday's terrible Quaker meeting which had gone so wrong; it was the occasion of great distress to me because Elders had done nothing to rescue it and I had not been quick enough to see what I should have done, which became clear to me a few days later. It is fairly rare for anyone to speak at the mid-week meetings but on this occasion someone said: 'One of the nice things about being a Quaker is that you do not have to wait until Christmas to bring gifts.' She added, almost as an after-thought: 'Including one's difficulties'. For some reason this completely set me off, and the tears came pouring down, and I could not stop them. I suppose it was the extraordinary coincidence that her words so met my condition since those were exactly the 'gifts' I had been bringing – although I had not thought of them as gifts. Actually, it is more than a coincidence that the lips of others speak for one in a Quaker meeting; it happens too often to be coincidence.

The third occasion which 'knocked the scab off' was Elizabeth's funeral, when the control in public was very difficult. For I was very fond of Elizabeth and had great admiration for her (having known her for 51 years, and she having been closely associated with Betty and myself over Pauline's birth, as well as being Susan's godmother). So the loss of Elizabeth was mixed up with the loss of Betty, and the whole pathos of ageing and so many contemporaries falling by the wayside … Susan's beautiful voice singing just beside me made it even harder.

That's another thing, not knowing how much the feeling tired, sleepy, disinclined to get up and do (which I seem to have suffered from a lot this week) is the result of grieving or just one of the uncomfortable effects of ageing. Yet one more of the confusions of my present state.

Earlier this week I went to the memorial service (Roman Catholic) for a friend and former colleague, and I did not take kindly to being urged to implore the Virgin Mary to intercede for his soul. At the reception afterwards, a compassionate and experienced lady G.P. of my acquaintance said: 'I understand that the second six months is worse than the first.' Does it really have to be? Oh God! The other day, when I was thinking upon the wise saying that bereavement can be a period of growth, the thought came to me that growth is a slow process.

In the case of Elizabeth's funeral, a Memorial Service at the church immediately followed the cremation two miles away. This was a big mistake, and much too soon; and the wrong time and place for the unctuous parson to be so hearty about saying it was an occasion for joy and tears should not be allowed. Of course he was quite right that it was an occasion for joy, in one sense, but the way he invoked it was crude, insensitive to the bereaved, and wrongly timed. He also made a big deal about the Resurrection, bouncing around and declaring that because of that everything was now all right. His vehemence did not convince me.

26 March 1994

This has been one of my worst weeks for a long time: so many tears, so much depression; it seems unfair to have both! Perhaps it is true that the second six months is worse than the first. Yet I *know* I have so many blessings.

Virginia pointed out that 'the second six months is worse' was only dealing in approximate time lengths. It is only in that sort of time scale that you can begin to take on board totally the whole meaning of the loss; and that is why the pain is bad. Necessarily bad, because you cannot go on to the next stage until you have been through the embracing of the whole loss. Virginia also said that she reckoned my tiredness, sleepiness, listlessness, disinclination to get up and do were the inevitable results of exhaustion and sorrow; no need to blame it on ageing; she repeated how tiring grieving was; no wonder I felt tired. Sorrow and exhaustion were entirely explicable and expected, but they were not really the same as real depression. My still wanting 48 hours in every twenty-four did not sound like a man suffering from depression. She also said it was good to listen to the Beethoven, the Liszt, the Grieg and other 'romantic' composers even if I knew it would produce the tears; it was good to go through the middle of all that even if painful, rather than duck it, until one could come out on the other side – however long it took. It was not emotional masturbation to do that, it was accepting the emotional part of me as it was at the moment.

28 March 1994

For some time I have been meaning to copy out an extract from Agnes Whitaker's anthology which has spoken for me so exactly; it is by Judy Tatelbaum:

"The death of a dear one is the most profound of all sorrows. The grief that comes with such a loss is intense and multi-faceted, affecting our emotions, our bodies, and our lives. Grief is preoccupying and depleting. Emotionally, grief is a mixture of raw feelings such as sorrow, anguish, anger, regret, longing, fear and deprivation. Grief may be experienced physically as exhaustion, emptiness, tension, sleeplessness, or loss of appetite. Grief invades our daily lives in many sudden gaps and changes, like that empty place at the dinner table, or the sudden loss of affection and companionship, as well as in many new apprehensions, adjustments and uncertainties. The loss of a dear one throws every aspect of our lives out of balance. The closer we were to the person who died, the more havoc the loss creates. Love does not die quickly. Hence to grieve is also 'to celebrate the depth of the union. Tears are then the jewels of remembrance, sad but glistening with the beauty of the past. So grief in its bitterness marks the end … but it is also praise to the one who is gone.'"

This line of thinking is a great consolation. Whenever I think I 'ought' to be making more 'progress' with my grief (in spite of Virginia Ross's denial of this) it is comforting to reflect that the very depth of my grief is proportional to the depth of our love; especially since being aware of the trap of beatification tends to make me cautious of looking at that love through rose-tinted spectacles. It is so hard to be honest. But it is some balm to have this assurance of the truth that 'We had so much, so much' – as I keep saying to Betty.

CHAPTER 3

The Second Six Months

1 April 1994

EXACTLY SIX MONTHS SINCE Betty died; and it so happens that this last week has been 'better', and there has been less of the grinding depression of the preceding month. I have asked myself if there is anything to which I can attribute this change. I think there could be three or four things. The first was undoubtedly the help of my hour-and-a-half with Virginia on Monday afternoon, which I think achieved the initial lift out of the gloom. The second was getting back to my project, which had been prevented by all sorts of busy-nesses since getting back from Derbyshire. Not only is preparing the book of extracts a slow, calming, creative occupation in itself, but this project is also 'doing something for Betty', so there are two sources of satisfaction in it. Thirdly, at the interment of Elizabeth Munnings's ashes on Tuesday, I managed to do satisfactorily the six-minute address I had been asked to give. At least, quite a number of people seemed to think it was satisfactory and said nice things afterwards, and that it just encapsulated Elizabeth appropriately. 'Very interesting and most unusual' said one man. 'Good' I said, 'then perhaps it was worthy of Elizabeth, because she was such an interesting and unusual person.' That of course had been my great anxiety, lest I might not do her justice. Incidentally, there was one interesting detail about the ceremony; the undertaker had covered up all the loose earth with that green matting they use, and I had noticed that with interest, assuming that this had been agreed and that therefore there would be no earth-throwing. But there was one lady there who was not to be denied, and obviously felt that her friend would not be properly sent on her way without it: she spoke to the undertaker, enquiring about earth, and then scrabbled about under the green matting for some, and sprinkled it onto the casket in lone determination. This custom of sprinkling earth on casket or coffin is one I have always hated, it has seemed unnecessarily ghoulish; it hit me first at my father's funeral, when the dear old parson conducting the ceremony made my mother have a good look at the coffin after it had

43

been lowered into the grave and throw earth on it. I suppose the idea is to underline that the person's body really is dead, really is returning dust to dust, really is laid to rest and will not return to haunt; the intention is to help people grasp the reality of the death. It is certainly dramatic, the earth thudding down with an awful finality. I can see that; but I still don't like it, and managed to arrange with the vicar that it was not done at the committal of Betty's ashes, although the undertaker disapproved of this since he regarded it as an omission of the proper ritual. Much more healing was the fact that all our children were there, and we were able to go back to my flat afterwards and have tea together on the patio in the autumn sunshine, chatting and laughing naturally.

In this week's *Friend* there's a bit about 'writing as bereavement therapy'. Apparently it seems to be a recognised technique. I hadn't heard of it before, I just stumbled into doing this by chance, as explained at the beginning. (Now I come to think of it – *was* it 'by chance?') Having started, I had this compulsion to go on; but I can recognise that it may have been therapeutic for me.

10 April 1994

I've definitely been 'better' this last fortnight, and have not been waking up so depressed. Doesn't mean that I haven't been reduced to tears when playing one of the Taizé tapes ... But again something contradictory in this 'better' situation: I hear two voices; when This Great Thing makes its presence felt, one voice says 'Don't pay any attention to that, you are better now, stay better, don't let yourself get upset again'; the other voice says guiltily 'How could you push the memory of Betty away from you like that?'. I just have to recognise that both voices are there.

I also find a slight change in meaning to my exclamations of 'Oh darling' which come out aloud quite spontaneously. Formerly they were just expressions of pure undifferentiated anguish; now there is sometimes something more matter-of-fact about them, something more of the 'Heigh-ho, well, darling, this is how it is'.

There is a new lady at Quaker Meeting, who lost her husband three months ago. Naturally I found myself talking to her and trying to be sympathetic. It seems that one of the things I said to her was: 'It's a strange country we find ourselves in, isn't it, one we've never been in before.' Apparently that struck something of a chord, because last Sunday she said she had been thinking about that phrase 'a strange country' all week.

I think I may have mentioned before that in some ways I felt I was becoming a different person as a result of all that has happened this last six months. When Pauline came to see me yesterday, quite spontaneously and with no prompting from me, she said the same thing of herself. She also told me something I had not known before. On the Tuesday, the day after Betty had been admitted to hospital, when I had spent some time in the morning with Betty having scraps of conversation and half-sentences and I then went home for lunch, Pauline came to visit Betty in her lunch hour. While Pauline was there Betty said 'I must go now', and Pauline was inclined to think she meant she needed to go to the loo or something. But in fact it was the last thing she said, because it was after that that she had her first 'fit'; thereafter she was in a coma until she died. Pauline also told me of a terrible dream she had had recently: in this dream Pauline was furiously angry with a whole lot of people, not with Betty although she was there, and Pauline vented her anger by kicking her mother, who thereupon dwindled into a small pile of bones. In her dream-sharing group Pauline was invited to play out this dream by taking the part of every person and object in it, as is the group's practice; when she was the bones she found she was not angry at all and said that being kicked had not hurt. Thank goodness for that, because understandably she had had a terrible time with the dream until it was exorcised in that way.

For five months my G.P. has been trying to get out of the NHS bureaucracy the final report from the hospital on Betty, and at last she has succeeded and sent it to me, inviting me to see her for her to explain any medical terms. The report does not really add anything to what we knew already, although it remains unclear *exactly* what happened – which were the real trigger factors, which came first in all the chickens and eggs of what Betty had wrong with her. This was why at the time the consultant had raised the question of having a post-mortem; which we declined, since he told me, in answer to my enquiry, that it would not really contribute to medical research, merely satisfy their curiosity to see if they had missed anything. My G.P. rather took me aback initially when she said it was remarkable that Betty was in hospital for such a short time, and I did not understand at first what she meant. She explained that in recent years Betty had had so much wrong with her and was 'failing' in so many respects that it was some achievement that I had managed to enable her to go on living independently at home for so long, and she reminded me of all the debates we had had about the various 'aids' which made that possible. It had never struck me that way, but it was comforting to hear the doctor say it. I suppose also, that because Betty had fought such a successful rearguard action for so many years, and we had done our best to cope with all her disabilities, that I had blinded myself to the possibility that hers was not a very good insurable life, and that she could not really have a great life expectancy. That was why her death came to me as a genuine shock.

In one sense seeing the medical report was of no importance; nothing more could be done now; I have no complaints about Betty's treatment in hospital, they could not have done more; the report did not answer any questions that had hitherto remained unanswered. Yet in another sense, having the report was of great importance to me – part of the 'completion' process, I suppose.

Virginia was pleased that I could report that the depression had not been so bad this last fortnight; but, without wishing to be discouraging, she warned me that it was always possible that I should plunge right down again – but, hopefully, never for quite so long or so far. A 'relapse' was always possible, but it did not have to be a total relapse. I arranged to see her again in a fortnight; I must say I was glad not to have to wait three weeks this time. The three weeks interval had been of my choice, because I had been afraid of becoming dependent on Virginia but now we had discussed it she did not think there was much danger of that and a fortnight was a better interval. We returned to the subject of guilt and I wondered whether I was being complacent and smug in not feeling guilt; she said 'Well, you don't *have* to feel guilt, it's just very common.' At a different point in the conversation I commented that I thought that, as a result of my experience, I understood more how women might have to grieve over a miscarriage; and said that I thought I was at the time less understanding of this and less sympathetic to Betty at the time of her miscarriages than I might have been. 'There's a bit of guilt for you if you want some!' she commented. Yet I'm still not sure that I feel that as guilt. Regret, yes; but guilt implies blaming myself; and at the time I don't think I had had enough experience, enough knowledge, and probably not enough imagination, to be really blameworthy for the omission.

23 April 1994

How I swing about still. This morning once more feels dull and down. Yet at last week's mid-week Meeting which I went to for an hour, I felt absolutely *showered* with blessings. But then, as I have mentioned before, there is a strange way in which the two things don't connect.

I think I am beginning to learn a bit more about this business of 'completing' one's grief – of letting the grief go without letting go of the love. The two can be separated; I had not seen that before. I haven't wept for a fortnight now; I almost wish I could.

When someone dies, the survivors commonly feel they have a lot of unfinished business with the deceased. It does not feel as if Betty and I had a lot of unfinished business – which perhaps means we were better prepared for her death than I realised. I thank God over and over again for the eighteen years of companionship and partnership we had after I retired from Ghana, when we were given all that time together.

Judy Tatelbaum quotes Bernard Shaw's 'Heartbreak is life educating us'.

25 April 1994

I find it is still helpful to go over and retell once again the story of Betty's dying, and in the last week I've had three such opportunities; I have grasped these with gratitude. The first was last Friday when I went up to see a Ghanaian friend of long standing before she left for Switzerland on her way back to West Africa, because I couldn't let her leave the country without seeing her. She had originally planned and very much wanted to come and visit Betty's grave, but she recovered more slowly than expected from her cataract operation and did not have time left to do so. When I was with her I suddenly realised that I had to tell her the full tale, and found myself more than willing to do so. The same when a friend of Betty's called in for coffee yesterday; and once more this morning when another friend called in, who only heard the bare fact a week ago.

I think I now have a greater understanding of the 'shock', or 'numbness', of the initial grieving period. What so many people describe as 'numbness', and which I did not feel I experienced, really has the same function as shock (which I did experience): namely, that in the early period, they both provide a kind of insulation against pain of such intensity that it would be unbearable or drive you mad if you did not have that protection. Then, as the shock or numbness begins to wear off, so the reality of the awful loss begins to hit you. Perhaps that is the explanation of the saying that the second six months is worse than the first. I certainly recognise the 'robot-like' way of functioning of the shock period – and the 'loss of self-confidence' of my present state, which apparently is also common.

2 May 1994

I was recently asked by a sympathetic friend: 'Are you now letting Betty go?', to which my answer was definitely 'No!' When I related this to Virginia, she said that it was too soon to expect this; she suggested that although my questioner had herself been through the experience of losing her husband she could well have forgotten how long it took for her to 'let him go': nature protects us from too painful memories. It can happen, eventually, in its own good time but it cannot be hurried. When it does happen, and you do 'let the beloved go', you can then re-possess her, inside you.

A lot of the time I nowadays go about with a 'facade' (e.g. 'Oh I'm fine, thanks' in reply to enquiries). Sometimes this feels hypocritical, but it is not, it is the necessity of intercourse with a wide variety of people. I told Virginia that I was consciously operating at two levels: the superficial facade, 'up here' (pointing to my forehead), and one's real feelings and preoccupations 'down here', in one's midriff. 'Exactly', she said, 'and with oceans of tears in between'. Actually, I have wept very little in the last three weeks; occasionally a particular piece of music has set the tears flowing, but no body-racking sobs as formerly. I sometimes wish I could have this relief, but I suppose it acts in the same way as any drug does to relieve pain; when you are coming off either you experience withdrawal symptoms. Instead of weeping I seem to go in for spontaneous long deep groans.

Judy Tatelbaum remains good reading. Like others she mentions sexuality, and how deeply it is affected by grief – confusion reigns: how right. The bereaved sometimes feel abandoned, or a victim of fate but I don't feel either of those. Nor has the experience made me have fresh questionings about my religion – I am accustomed to such questionings being a continuous process anyway. Nor has it resulted in an intensification of wondering what happens after death; Betty's has just fitted into whatever patterns of belief/disbelief I had before. I recognise being off-balance, with the danger of doing self-destructive things, which I therefore try to guard against. I recognise, too, the difficulty of changing habits, particularly verbal ones. I still tend to say 'We have four children'; I suppose to say 'I' would feel like letting Betty go, and I am resisting that; yet when I say 'we' or 'I', I tend to feel self-conscious about it, because neither is right. I find it very difficult to refer to Betty's dog Dancer as 'my' dog. It is said that we are moving closer to recovering from grief when the deceased is no longer our primary focus. I am sure that is true, but all I can say is that Betty still remains my primary focus quite definitely. Once again, I suppose it must be too soon to expect that particular change. Another sign of entering the final stage of grief is said to be when we look to our future and reinvest in our life. But again, I'm not yet ready for that; I move from one thing to the next, as it comes along. I am not planning my life ahead – except perhaps in relation to two vague ideas. One is to write these notes up properly – which have now become part of the coming-to-terms-with-the-grief process, trying to accept the reality. The other idea is nothing new, but something which several people (including Betty) put to me before she died, which is to write my memoirs or an autobiography. But I don't see myself starting on that one until the first one is done, and not on that until the 'Betty book' project is completed.

6 May 1994

Our society does not help the bereavement situation because of the way it instills false notions of courage – it is 'courageous' to be silent when in pain, to control tears at all costs, to continue to function in spite of the turmoil going on inside. I am frequently aware that I expect myself to function in spite of the inner turmoil. One result is that some people grieve in secret. I don't grieve in secret, but I do choose to do my grieving in private. Additional 'pressure' at such a time can become intolerable. When a transatlantic friend wrote and asked me 'to be nice' to a visiting American student, I was incapable of doing anything about it. The bereaved should not be pressed about their future – which sympathetic enquirers often do, knowing there is a big change in circumstances.

Although it is hard to believe, I think I do have faith that we *can* recover from our sorrow. Tatelbaum has good things to say on this. Recovery from our grief is said to be the restoration of our capacity for living a full life and enjoying life without feelings of guilt, shame, sorrow or regret. We have recovered when we once again feel able to cope with our feelings and our environment, and when we can face reality and accept our loss on a gut level, not just intellectually. Integrating our loss and reinvesting in our lives constitutes recovery. It is asserted that the depth of sorrow, the pain, the weeping, the incapacitation, the neediness, and all the intense feelings of mourning eventually diminish and disappear. 'We do not forget the deceased or the loss, but the pain recedes. Usually the dissolving of grief is gradual rather than sudden. In the process of recovering, grief may be triggered unexpectedly many times before completion. We may go through different waves of pain, until the waves stop coming. Once we recover, the gap left by the loss may still be evident but our reactions to it will be less intense.'

Recovery is said to result from setting recovery as an essential goal and from living each day as it comes. Well, I am very definitely living each day as it comes, and have been for some time now, but I have not 'set recovery as an essential goal' – at least not consciously. But I do have faith that recovery can and will happen – and I am prepared to let it happen, in its own good time. I am now *willing* to let the pain gradually diminish (as in the recovery of a broken arm), and am now prepared to let go of my resistance to the fading of the pain, which I know I formerly had. This is possible because I now know that the pain can go while the loss and the memories and the love remain.

Yesterday a very good friend called in who knew Betty and myself pretty well. She surmised that I might be missing the whole of my life with Betty, the negative things as well as the positive things. I could agree with this, because it is the whole partnership and companionship, the

difficulties and the wearinesses as well as the happinesses and ease which
are lost. She instanced Betty's habit of 'putting me down' in public (a
habit which Betty learnt to think was all right from her mother's example
to her) and which she needed to boost her own precarious self-confidence.
While I acknowledged it was so, and that sometimes this irritated me, I
had come to terms with it and was so used to it that it became like water
off a duck's back. Consequently I had not been aware that this was one
of the things I was missing. But it is quite right that it is the total package
which constitutes the loss.

11 May 1994

Had another session with Virginia at the beginning of the week, and
there occurred one of those sudden and unexpected waves of grief. She
had been asking whether birthdays and anniversaries were difficult, and
I was able to say 'Not really'. I explained how I was trying to keep up
taking notice of the family's birthdays (only in the form of a birthday card)
from the notes of them in Betty's diary; and that I had managed to do
Christmas presents (for which Betty had always done the thinking) in a
comparatively matter-of-fact and objective sort of way. 'I was really
thinking of Betty's birthday, and your birthday' said Virginia. 'No', I said,
'those went all right. The children were very good to me on both occasions.' Then I suddenly added, quite without premeditation, I really do
not know what shot it into my mind, 'What is difficult is the spring flowers
coming on the patio' – and the picture suddenly had me weeping copiously. Virginia, bless her, of course knew what to do: precisely nothing,
and say nothing. She just let me be with it, and I knew I could be, and
did not feel I had to hurry myself to 'pull myself together'. I think it was
the first time I had wept properly for a month. I said to her afterwards:
'Why is it that when someone is weeping our instinct is to say "Don't
cry?"' (which of course she had NOT said). 'Oh', she said, 'it is because
we cannot bear *our* pain at seeing the other person's pain; we are thinking
of ourselves. We are saying "Please don't hurt me with your pain".'

After leaving Virginia I had to go out to dinner, and suddenly change
gear to the upper, outer 'façade' level; I gave myself a bit of time sitting
in the car to make the transition. In the next morning's post there was a
tape of the Fauré Requiem from a friend. so naturally I put it on. Following
on the spring flowers of the previous day, it collapsed me completely and
the tears flowed even more copiously than twelve hours before; perhaps
it was really all part of the one outburst of grief: not having had one for
a month, then I have two, the second prolonged and violent, in twelve
hours!

Then against all this – the blessings! No – not *against* all this, but *with* all this. A friend had asked me to get hold of an autobiographical book by a college contemporary of mine because his father had been Rector of a small village in Kent where she had taught during the war and with whom she had fire-watched. I came to know of this because of this contemporary's obituary in the college Annual, which mentioned the name of the village. This man and I were not exact contemporaries, he came up a year after I did; now he was dead, and I, a year older, survived. My life is now very well worth living, in spite of the grief. Can I not then be grateful for every day I am given, which he is not? The strange mixture still; I do often have a measure of depression when I wake up, but I can also look forward to what the day coming holds for me and the things which I shall enjoy. Is this not a gift? The last two weeks I have got on well with my 'Betty book' project and this is immensely satisfying; at the beginning of each day I have been able to think pleasurably about the next bit that I am going to be able to get on with.

19 May 1994

This has been the worst fortnight for ages, because there has been a return of the most grinding depression, which seems unaccountable, unless it is just the rhythm of the thing. I sometimes feel as if I am paralysed. My loss and Betty's absence are still totally dominant in my consciousness. Today I have the great satisfaction of having at last finished the book project. Yet I do not feel the real elation over this that I should; too tired, perhaps.

Nevertheless there was one very good and, I think, 'progressive' thing which happened a week ago. I went to see Helen, who put me off the last time I phoned before proposing a visit as her sleep pattern had changed and she was sleeping all day and waking all night, I suppose to do with her illness. Anyway I spent nearly two hours with her this time, and discovered a new person whom I had not encountered before – the person that Betty was so close to. I had not before realised how close. Helen said that she used to talk about spiritual things to her, and there was no one else she could do that with. So I can see how much Helen misses Betty too.

I had just come from the university library, where I had been trying to arrange for two copies of a Ph.D. thesis to be made to send to two West African universities. It was disgraceful that the author had never sent a single copy to anyone or any institution in West Africa when he completed it over four years ago, although he had 'mined' West African sources for it to benefit his own career. So I have been very indignant about that for a long time anyway, especially as he was a student of mine. A fortnight ago I made enquiries in the university library about the conditions for copying, was told that author's permission was no longer required. So this time I went just to place the order, now knowing what it would cost me. At the relevant desk I encountered an unhelpful official who produced different regulations from those I had been told before; when I complained of the difference he told me it was my fault for having asked the wrong questions. I was so livid I found it difficult not to resort to abuse, and to exit with any sort of dignity.

So I came to Helen still seething. She was very sympathetic, but pointed out, when I had said that I had not felt anger over Betty's death, that grief involves all the emotions, including anger, and it does not have to be directly connected with the death or the dead person; so that the extreme measure of my anger was, in fact, probably part of my grieving.

I have also felt angry with Joyce, of whom I am very fond, because of the way she tries to organise my life. The other night, when I answered the phone, she said aggressively: 'What does that tone of voice mean?' She went on to enquire 'how I was', and then said accusingly 'Are you low?' All meant kindly, and out of caring concern, but it makes me angry. I think Joyce thinks it would be 'good for me' to have all sorts of occupations and busy-ness, I have more than enough to do, I still want 48 hours in the 24, but I do not want to be told what to do. I have been very troubled over this business with Joyce, because I have great admiration for her and I love her dearly, and I'm terrified of having a bust-up with her on the telephone when she makes me so angry, and I'm frightened of saying something I might regret. So I have been asking myself *why* it makes me so angry; and I think that this morning I worked out some of the answer: which is that this sort of behaviour by Joyce threatens me being able to be myself in my grieving; I know I need to grieve, and doing my own things enables me to, and is part of the process; being made to do different things, against what I want to do, is almost like *preventing* me going on with my grieving. You see, I do not know whether Joyce, for all her care, thinks that by now 'I ought to have got over it.'

(One of the things Helen said when I was discussing with her how long it would take to reach something called 'recovery', was that there was no rule of thumb, in spite of the guidelines the books gave. 'It will take you as long as it takes', she said.)

So next time Joyce rubs me up the wrong way, out of a misunderstanding of the grief process, I must try to have the patience not to react with a great flare of anger, but with a quiet assertiveness of my own position; and not feel defensive, as she tends to make me, because she is a very insistent, persuasive and determined person. In talking about other people sharing one's grief, Helen said that their sharing has to be completely non-intrusive; how right she is, and how non-intrusive she herself is. It requires sensitivity. Joyce's concern is apt to be intrusive.

Helen, who is a member of *Mensa*, said: 'Betty was lovely; she was clever and she was wonderful.' I picked upon the word 'clever', because it was correct, but Helen is the only one who has ever used that word of her; I blessed her for doing so and recognising the fact, which was not so apparent to others; and we talked about just what 'clever' meant in Betty's case.

Helen has helped me to grieve as no one else has except Virginia; with the result that on one occasion the tears were copious but I was not ashamed of them or felt the need to hide or restrain them: a tribute to Helen. When I thanked her at the end, I commented on how much she knew without having actually experienced the loss of a partner, and how much wisdom I felt she had. She reminded me that she had a degree in psychology! But that is no guarantee of wisdom!

In bed this morning the following verse emerged:

> She has suffered a fold catastrophe,
> Irreversible, yet more like a phase change;
> Mine is different, and I must range
> Through all grief's cusp polyphony.

23 May 1994

An acquaintance of Betty's and mine called in yesterday and talked about the Gestalt method of therapy for the bereaved, by persuading them to talk to the dead person in an empty chair, especially about the negative things in the relationship; which they say it is necessary to deal with before you can let the dead person go. I have accepted that the finishing process is necessary, but I know I am not yet ready consciously to embark on this. I'll let it come when it comes. I felt that my visitor was rather inclined to force the pace, to regard the book project as 'unhealthy beatification', possibly even dishonest and hypocritical (although she did not actually use any of those words). She reminded me of the difficulties I had had with Betty, of which she knew something because she had asked me to be a guinea-pig as the subject of a case-study for part of her psychotherapy training. Some seven months ago she shocked me by asking me within a month of Betty's death whether I was beginning to enjoy my new-found freedom. I replied at the time: 'It's too soon to think about that', and she should have known that as well. Quite right to help a person start recognising the advantages of things like that when they are reaching the third stage of grief and are beginning to 'finish' and let go, but not in the midst of the very acute first stage of anguish. I was angry with her and felt that she did not realise how much Betty and I had had together; the tensions between us were all part of it, and that is part of the loss too. Betty and I managed to keep our marriage going in spite of the tensions, because we knew there was value in it in spite of those tensions, and we had our rewards; this lady's situation is quite different: she is quitting her marriage and is revelling in her new-found freedom. She did not appreciate the nature of my and Betty's relationship; she only saw the negative aspects; and she herself did not like Betty personally. I am well aware of the dangers of the false idealisation of a dead person but I am not going to make the mistake in the opposite direction and throw the baby out with the bath water; just because of my awareness of the danger of idealisation, I am not going to deny all the positive things that are there. 'Love' is a word I fight shy of, because it can mean such a multitude of different things, and is so sugared over with sentimentality. Betty quite often wanted an assurance that I loved her and I found this difficult to express in words; it was easier to do so in action. I *valued* her, and tried to cherish her, but she wanted the verbal assurances – all part, I suppose, of her lack of self-confidence.

In my fortnightly session with Virginia we somehow got onto Betty's jealousy of the children. I explained how I no longer had to look over my shoulder at Betty's jealousy, and that therefore my relationship with my children had changed. Somehow also there was mention of Betty's repeatedly saying she was 'a difficult woman', as if that excused anything, until I finally said to her 'And that's nothing to be proud of!' Virginia brought up the difficulties arising out of Betty's illness and disability; I acknowledged these difficulties, although at the time these did not loom large for me. To have let them would have hindered getting on with the business of helping – although I admitted there was sometimes a conflict between compassion and irritation. I conceded that in order to 'finish' the grieving process, it might be necessary for me to deal with the negative side of Betty and my relationship with her but I did not feel ready to do that yet. Virginia pointed out 'But you've already begun to do that! This is the first time with me that you have done that, and mentioned such things as the jealousy, the 'difficult woman' and the 'disability difficulties'.

29 May 1994

Eight months since Betty died. I spent a few days with Richard and his family. They were very kind, although there was not much opportunity to talk about Betty's death. I brought it up in conversation once or twice, as opportunity offered. However, there was not really any chance to follow it up, although I never got the feeling that anyone was shying away from it. I think Richard is better able to cope than any of the others, because I think he has 'done' the grief over the loss they suffered some years ago.

At home last night I just felt so tired, so tired from all this grieving, to the extent that I shouted it at my pillow: 'I'm so tired, so tired, so *tired*'. It is a strange sort of tiredness, too; partly physical, but predominantly emotional I suppose, certainly not the lack-of-sleep sort of tiredness. A sort of inertness. Physically it seems to be accompanied by a lot of sighs.

Betty 'spoke to me in a dream' last night. I have been thinking quite a lot about the negative side of her character and the negative side of our relationship, as the books say is necessary if the grief is to be completed. There is the elaboration of this idea of not only thinking about these negative aspects, but also of confronting Betty with them in an empty chair opposite. I do not feel ready for that yet, and feel reluctant to attempt it (in any case it may need help), even if I can at the moment start thinking about it. The books also speak about the need for forgiveness. In this dream, Betty was defensive and highly indignant that there was anything for which I needed to forgive her.

I do not find it difficult to contemplate my own death – what I know I have found difficult is to accept the reality, the fact, of Betty's. Thinking about this, I found myself saying aloud emphatically 'Betty is *dead!*'. By all accounts this should represent some sort of 'progress'; I know I have not been able to do that before.

5 June 1994

I think this is the worst yet. I really do feel as if I am 'dragging my life from numbered stone to numbered stone'. Last night and this morning I have several times cried out R.H. Benson's 'prayer after crushing bereavement' (quoted by Whitaker) 'Oh Lord, have pity on this darkened soul of mine!'. Music still tips me over. This morning Tchaikowsky's 'Waltz of the Flowers' from the Nutcracker Suite really did it, and had me flinging myself into a chair, shouting and shouting through my tears and beating my thighs. Am I over-dramatising to myself? Should I control such spontaneous expressions? I've been told that it is good to give rein to the natural expressions of one's grief, but does the point come when one has done it enough? Does it spontaneously stop, or does one have to take a hand in making it do so?

By chance I met Betty's consultant in the lift at the hospital yesterday when visiting a friend. I was able to repeat my thanks to him and his colleagues for all that they did last October. At the end of our conversation he said 'And how are you?'. 'Oh, I'm serving out my sentence', I said.

He gave a little chuckle of surprise at the expression, and then added 'I know what you mean'. Virginia also liked the phrase, but I pointed out the difference from a prison sentence that with bereavement one did not know how long the sentence was going to be. I think this is one of my biggest difficulties at the moment.

The extraordinary non-contacting juxtaposition of anguish and blessings continues, with both very much in the forefront of my consciousness. I have never known such anguish, and I cannot recall ever being aware of so many blessings; yet the blessings do not ameliorate the anguish, the anguish does not detract from the blessings. I do *not* feel inclined to say of the blessings 'Oh they don't count really, they don't really make any difference'; nor can I believe that the anguish could be any greater if I did not have the blessings. I just don't know; all part of the confusion. I told Virginia that I could not tell whether my tirednesses, weaknesses and disinclinations were the result of ageing or of grief. She said she would bet that they were 80% grief, since the coping with conflicting emotions was so exhausting. Is my saying 'I have never been aware of so many blessings', a nudge towards something I should learn from this experience? Should I henceforth always be conscious of (and therefore grateful for) my blessings to a greater extent than I have been hitherto?

Yesterday I had a lovely letter from Sister Mary, in the course of which she said, referring to Betty: '... it came to me on Christmas Eve that with her dying she became all yours once again, just as the day when you were married. All through her life, and more and more I would think just latterly you have had to share her with so many others – yet that essential core, the Betty that only *you* know, remains yours.' Perceptive of Sister Mary to see what 'sharing Betty' meant for me, and what the not having to do so now can also mean.

6 June 1994

In the pit. Waiting – waiting to get out of it. Not knowing whether I have to wait for this to happen, or whether I have to make violent efforts to scramble out myself. I suppose I ought to be able to wait 'patiently', but I do not seem able to do that. Curiously, there is an article in this week's *Friend* on waiting, in which the sentence occurs: 'The tension, or lack of it, is intolerable ...' How it is. The words of the 131st Psalm happened to fall under my eyes: 'O Lord, ... I am not concerned with great matters or with subjects too difficult for me. Instead I am content and at peace.' Content, yes, I am, but I am far from being at peace.

I thought of the last time I experienced prolonged depression – in 1974, when I was not only suffering from the culture-shock of returning from West Africa but was also in considerable financial difficulty; this was the result, as I saw it, of being cheated on every one of the five sources of income on which I had calculated I should be able to retire at 60. Anger and loss. The comparison gave me the perception that I have not only lost the person of Betty, which hitherto I have thought of as the whole loss, but also of the state and achievement of our marriage. Just as in 1974 I felt robbed of the financial state I should have been in and of the achievement of getting there, so now I have lost the enormous investment which Betty and I put into our marriage; because the emotional and practical investment in that 53 years was indeed enormous. I suppose that cannot disappear overnight without it being felt as a loss, although I had not hitherto identified it as such, because the personal one is so much greater.

15 June 1994

I've read in the newspaper lately about 'Post-trauma Stress Condition', and how long-lasting it can be, especially if the victim does not receive the right sort of help. God, I can understand that now. Bereavement of this intensity constitutes a trauma all right – using 'trauma' in its correct medical meaning, not in the popular misuse of it which has come about in recent years, to mean simply something unpleasant. Another newspaper report spoke about the survivors of the Hillsborough disaster, and the counselling they had received: many of the men refused to accept such counselling on the grounds that to do so would be displaying 'weakness' and they felt they should be strong enough to cope on their own. I know how they felt. Grateful as I am for my sessions with Virginia, and much as I acknowledge I have needed them and have benefited from them, nevertheless I know that with some people I have concealed the fact that I have been having this help. I guess this is an indication of how much I am still under the tyranny of the inner need to conform to the male macho image.

All part of the 'facade' too, I think. Hearing someone refer to how Betty was wont to show a cheerful face to most people in spite of her pain and disability, I wondered whether there was positive virtue in my being a good actor with those who would themselves be distressed if they had to face evidence of my sorrow. The first part of this sentence raises another of the nasty 'negative' thoughts about Betty – whether 'showing a cheerful face in spite of her pain and disability' was the message people were supposed to take away with them, rather than *just* showing a cheerful face, and keeping the pain and disability to herself. How nasty can I be? But I know this is what some people thought – and that she used her disability as a weapon. There! I've said it.

One of the many things I miss her for is talking about the problems of ageing, which we shared quite a lot. I have recently had distressing evidence of my increasing senility, in remembering nothing about some negotiations I had fifteen and more years ago with the Smithsonian Institution in Washington and the Corning Museum of Glass who have now reactivated a research programme using samples I provided them with; I accused them of using my samples without my permission, until they sent me copies of my own correspondence! Another thing: I was asked to produce some sentences for the scientific correspondent of the *Independent* saying what was new and revolutionary about the book I have been editing; I tried, but without a copy of the book in front of me (it is at the printers) I found I could not do it. Formerly I should have been able to get some sympathy from Betty about this disability on my part – even if she tried to persuade me that it did not matter.

25 June 1994

It has been getting a bit 'better', lately. I had a good weekend in Derbyshire doing another art course. We had a very good teacher, quite unorthodox, a bit too 'jokey' (as opposed to witty) and opinionated; I should find him tedious after more than two days, but for a short course one can take it. For a lot of the two days I was able to forget 'the Big Thing', being totally absorbed for a couple of hours at a time in the drawing. Such absorption is quite different from 'being occupied' (which everyone wishes on me), for in all the daily occupations, and many others, the 'Big Thing' is still there.

Another good session with Virginia. I told her I was still shying away from looking at the negative sides of Betty's character, and mine, and in our marriage – particularly this idea of 'confronting' her with these things in an empty chair in front of me. Is it not enough to recall them, and acknowledge them, by setting them down here? I remember a particularly unpleasant and irritating habit of Betty's, which was her sneer, sometimes accompanied by a positive snort, and often with an icily keen cutting edge to her voice. She employed it quite often on me, but I cannot recall hearing her doing it to other people; she used it particularly on me to indicate she did not believe me – as when I said I had been to the University Library and she believed I had been seeing a friend. She always expected me to give an account of my movements, an accounting which she did not always choose to reciprocate. That, of course, was something which maddened me with the unfairness of it: she would get nasty over my doing something with someone else which she regarded as perfectly all right when she did the same thing with David M. The independence which I accorded her she did not want to accord to me; that was one of the reasons why it was constructive to put some space between us for a time in the third decade of our marriage.

Virginia said at one point 'You did an awful lot for Betty', to which my natural reaction was 'Oh, I don't know, not all that much.' But Virginia insisted that I must have. I do know that in recent years, as Betty's disabilities got worse, I consciously said to myself that looking after and cherishing her was my principal job and top priority. Some of this was in the realm of thinking about and anticipating her needs as well as doing the physical things. I already know about the need to love yourself if you are to be able to love other people, but Virginia added 'And forgive yourself' and 'Accept yourself'. I think there is probably quite a lot in what she says in this context.

I've at last begun sorting through some of Betty's papers, partly because I am a bit less busy now (book tribute completed, edited book actually published), and also because I feel strong enough to tackle it. I came across some letters Betty had had from two convent Sisters at the time of her operations and afterwards (1985,6) with words of comfort for her physical and spiritual sufferings. Sister Mary produced one new metaphor which leapt out of the page at me as applicable to my present desolation: 'One simply has to huddle as in a sandstorm until gradually one begins to come out of it.'

28 June 1994

I've just realised I am beginning to try to find my new identity. This is always something of a problem for people when a big change occurs in their lives. A child has the identity which is largely given to him, adolescents have the difficult job of finding a new identity as they are entering into adulthood; this is where initiation ceremonies make the process much easier in pre-literate societies; in ours we make the process much more difficult by leaving adolescents to sort it out for themselves. Because she was so dominated by her mother in her childhood and youth, one of Betty's difficulties was that all her life she was trying to discover her identity, and she herself was aware of this. Your identity is what you are, but it is so easy to confuse it with what you do. I realise also that it is not only a question of *finding* your identity, as if it was something already existent 'out there' and you merely had to pluck it out of the air, it is also very much a question of *creating* your identity from what you 'really' are, without being led away by other people into things which are not really 'you'. Before my 1962 crash I thought I was happy with my identity as husband and responsible father, as a supporter of my parish church, and as someone earning his daily bread in something called 'education', about which I became more and more disillusioned. Then after my crisis I suddenly had to create for myself an identity as a university professor and as someone separated from his family for three-quarters of the year. To start with, doing the professor bit was only achieved as a conscious piece of bluff. It was only later that I knew I was doing it competently, and getting inner satisfaction from this, and from making research discoveries which seemed to me to be more genuine and worthwhile than the charlatanism which prevailed in the field of 'Education'. But I had to grow to this, and it meant a big change of identity by the time the process was complete.

Now my circumstances have changed, with Betty's death, and this means that my identity can change from having been 'Betty's carer'; from having been seen as such, and having thought of myself as such. I am only just beginning to realise this. In a way there is additional change, too, because for almost twenty years I have been 'one who was so dedicated to his academic discipline that he did as much in retirement as ever before.' For six or seven years after I left full-time employment in my overseas university that was true, and I had the energy and interest for it to be so. That was broken by my stroke, and I was quite content to let all that go, once I had written up for publication all my fieldwork. But then I was dragged out of that more real retirement by being asked to run a section of an international conference and to edit its papers – a commitment which has unexpectedly continued until today because that undertaking became expanded into the creation of an enormous volume, with three changes of publishers on the way. Now that the book is actually out at last, I hope I can really let all that run down. In the last twelve months I have succeeded in saying 'No' to two pressing requests to write major contributions in collaborative works. So that should leave me freer from that sphere.

But it is only in relation to 'no longer being Betty's carer' that I have realised the glimmerings of a new identity – what one might call a 'post-Betty' identity. I think this must represent progress in the *cursus doloris*, the curriculum of grieving. There are pangs and anguish and a temptation to guilt in this realisation, but I am not paying too much attention to the latter as I know that Betty herself would think it was 'a good thing'.

So what is my new identity going to be? What am I seeking? What am I looking for? What am I trying to construct?

29 June 1994

Yesterday I wrote 'One of Betty's difficulties was that all her life she was trying to find her identity, and she was aware of this.' I had been thinking about this, and reflecting that in her later years she really did seem to have succeeded. Now comes the strange coincidence (??). Today I was going through some of her papers, and came across the following autobiographical bit, written in her own handwriting:

"When I reached the grand age of 50 I remember thinking that NOW was the moment to look into the future and to consider what lay before me. At that time, 2 daughters had recently married and there were 2 sons and a daughter who were still more or less home based. My husband had about 8 years to go before retiring. Suddenly, six years later, all the birds had flown from the nest, my 'oldies' whom I had nursed, loved and cared for had both died within 6 months of each other and I realised that NOW had truly arrived when I must find ME – not the Prof.'s wife, the children's mother, anybody's daughter, the grandchildren's substitute Mum but my own self.

This was the moment when I needed to assess my interests, my possibilities and my problems – we all have to do this sooner or later and it can be a very salutary exercise. My problems appeared manifold or so it seemed. To begin with I had been poorly-educated, and following a horrific riding accident at 17 which put me out of action for a year, I had done dietetic nursing of sick babies, because I adored babies. After marrying at 22 and bearing and rearing 4 children, I developed arthritis – problem No 2. You learn to live with considerable pain, it is not something which you can ignore. Sitting or standing in any one position for very long is difficult, so these were my main problems.

My interests I was able to sort out fairly easily. I love listening to music and studying art. I read a good deal and have a particular interest in religion; stillness and quietness mean a great deal to me. So with my problems and interests before I was in a position to discover my possibilities ..."

Betty goes on to describe the steps which led to her embarking on an Open University course, and then to relate her experience of doing the first year of it – but she closes the account before knowing the result of her first year exam. (which in fact she passed). This document would make moving reading for anybody, but Betty being the writer, it absolutely bowled me over. (I have often told people, previously, how intensely moving I found it seeing the flowering of intellectual excitement in Betty as she did her O.U.course.) I have been weeping and weeping and I let myself go with it completely, in a strange mixture of anguish and joy. Mind you, you could say that I had already been 'softened up' for this yesterday, when, in going through Betty's things, I came across the notebook she started before we were married, listing her trousseau, our wedding presents etc, and I found that she had stuck in the flyleaf the following poem:

A SONG OF THE ROAD

Oh, I will walk with you my lad, which ever way you fare
You'll have me to the side of you, with heart as light as air;
No care for where the road you take's a-leading anywhere –
It can but be a joyful jaunt the while you journey there.
The road you take's the path of love, an' that's the breadth of two,
And I will walk with you, my lad – oh, I will walk with you.

> *Oh, I will walk with you, my lad,*
> *Be weather black or blue,*
> *Or roadsides frost or dew, my lad –*
> *Oh, I will walk with you.*

Ay, glad, my lad, I'll walk with you, whatever winds may blow,
Or summer blossoms stay our steps, or blinding drifts of snow;
The way that you set face and foot's the way that I will go,
And brave I'll be, abreast of you, the saints and angels know.
With loyal hand in loyal hand, and one heart made of two,
Through summer's gold, or winter's cold, it's I will walk with you.

> *Sure, I will walk with you, my lad,*
> *As love ordains me to,*
> *To heaven's door, and through my lad;*
> *Oh, I will walk with you.*

James Whitcomb Riley

Is it any wonder that that set me weeping? The first time for about
four weeks. Typing it out now has done it again.

It set me off again, of course, when going through a folder of Betty's
notes on dying and bereavement (which up to that point I had been able
to do quite dry-eyed, selecting what was worth keeping, what not) when
I found she had kept a copy there of that incredibly beautiful poem of
D.H. Lawrence's, "Shadows" which I am very fond of and love anyway –
but reading it again in that context collapsed me completely.

Having read Betty's own account of her trying to find *and construct*
her identity, I am quite certain she consciously went through a similar
process after she had completed her O.U. course; and that is how her
counselling and spiritual guiding came to take on a more formalised and
regular pattern.

I have been in no hurry to move into Betty's room, as of course it involves going through all her things, but a week or so ago I felt I was ready for it, and made a beginning. I felt able to – although I knew it might happen that some things would 'set me off' again. I think I was doing pretty well, actually, and realised it was necessary if I was ever going to be able to 'complete my grief'.

3 July 1994

It is now nine months since Betty died.

In going through Betty's papers I came across a page torn out of *The Friend* of 31 August 1984, where Sally Juniper reviews a book by Dr Tony Lake called 'Living with Grief'. It sounds fairly good, and might even have one or two new lines. Two landmarks in 'progress' he notes: when you can hear other people refer to the dead person without needing to add information, take over the conversation or correct wrong impressions; and when you make a new friend who only knew you in your present state. I don't think I have reached either of those landmarks yet!

Another of Betty's sets of notes, on a course on Bereavement quotes two well-known things, but which I think are worth repeating here:

'The pain of grief is the cost of love.'

'The grief of bereavement is an experience for life ... one never loses it.'

I went to see Helen again – who I realise more and more was deeply close to Betty, I don't think I had realised before how close. Helen told me that Betty had said to her that she felt she had not given me the support I needed when I was so depressed ('near-breakdown', Betty had called it) when suffering the combination of culture-shock in returning from my overseas university, and financial worries and anxieties when I felt I had been cheated on five sources of income on which I had counted; I indulged in a lot of self-pity. I know at the time I felt I received little sympathy from Betty, who seemed to be taking the line that material things did not matter and that I was being very worldly to be so worried, whereas she had a more spiritual faith that everything would be all right. Betty told Helen that she thought that was the best way to handle me at the time, but she later realised it was not the most helpful attitude. Betty never told me this, and I am grateful to have it now through Helen.

In one of Betty's notes on bereavement, it cites denial of anger as typical of 8-9 months! Helen said I still needed to be able to express my anger at Betty's death – not with Betty for deserting me but at Life for doing this to me. She said confidently that the anger was there but that I couldn't express it, and suggested that it was blocked by my continuing anger at my mother. I had told her all that tale. Psychotherapy had taken me a long way along that path, but I don't think I was ever able to confront my mother and say 'I hate you'; and I told Helen I could not now. Is it not rather a need to recognise all the terrible things my mother did to me, and which affected my life so deeply, and of then *forgiving* her? Of recognising that what she did may have been mistaken, but that it was done in love, in the belief that it was what was best for me? Is it necessary to go through an expression of hatred in order to fully recognise those terrible things before attempting the path of forgiveness? I denied feeling anger at Life for the loss of Betty, because I reckoned I had had a good life and had had more joys and blessings than sorrows and disasters, and therefore the pain of Betty's loss did not seem 'unfair'. Helen said she did not think in fact that I had had more joys than sorrows, and that it was a case of selective memory burying many of the sorrows. 'Look at your childhood' she said 'which you have looked upon as "a happy childhood". It was a miserable childhood!' Psychologists who tell people to say 'I hate my mother' should not do that. What they can do is to tell people to say 'I love my mother and I hate her too.'

I read somewhere recently: 'When your life is in transition, you will be in psychological turmoil.' I suppose I am now in the biggest process of transition for over fifty years; I know there were big transitions when we first came home from West Africa; again three years later when we moved house to a different village; I had a new job, and Betty fell in love with a new man; again eight years later, when I fell in love with a new woman; again six years later when I had a breakdown and began an overseas job. When I retired from there and came back to England was another transition, and again when we moved to this flat six months before Betty died. These were all big transitions – but in all of them, Betty was there. Now the transition is to life without her; that's why I think I am justified in calling it my biggest transition for over fifty years. No wonder I am in psychological turmoil.

12 July 1994

This grief of bereavement seems to spawn metaphors. Because there is just nothing like it, I suppose it is only by metaphor one can approach describing it. Another metaphor has occurred to me in the last day or two: before a pilot can get his licence, he has to log so many hours solo flying time; in the same way, I think it may be that before one can 'complete one's grieving', one has to put in so many hours of weeping. If that is so, I have been doing well this last fortnight! Following, curiously enough, three or four weeks when I did not weep at all. I think two things have triggered it: the first is that I have at last got round to going through all the things in Betty's room. I got Pauline and Susan to deal with all Betty's clothes a week or ten days after she died, and soon after, I distributed all the pieces of specified jewellery to our daughters, daughters-in-law and grand-daughters according to the list Betty and I had agreed before she died; everything else I left untouched. Now my stimulus is that it would be so much less trouble to have a separate desk or table for drawing instead of always having to remove all the things on my writing and business desk, as I have had to do hitherto. I plan to have such a table or desk in what was Betty's room, as it has so much better light; and also to use that room as my bedroom because it would be wicked for that lovely window looking out on the fields to go unused. So to do all this involves going through all Betty's things, including remaining jewellery, all her personal things, all her papers. Having spent the last two or three weeks doing this has also enabled me to start giving all the female members of the family a pick at the remaining jewellery, and to invite a number of her friends to see if there is anything of Betty's they would like to have. So far this has gone very well and all concerned seem very pleased. Naturally I haven't given them free range, but have reserved certain things for myself.

I was able to embark on this process of going through Betty's things in quite a matter-of-fact and objective sort of way; it was just the next thing that had to be done, but I knew that there would be some things that would just tip me over. I was not wrong. That would be enough explanation for my being so weepy this last fortnight. The other thing has been further getting back to music: Beethoven, of course, who more than any other can reduce me to tears anyway, the Violin Concerto and the Romances 1 and 2. Then Mozart's *Eine Kleine Nachtmusik*, which has now become so popular – but this time I was hearing it for the first time with Betty at a concert by the Cape Town Municipal Orchestra when on leave there in 1940; I was enchanted on that occasion, and Betty and I shared our common enthusiasm.

It is strange but perhaps this new round of weeping is a bit different from before, because as well as being the natural outcome of the pain of loss, I think that also it may, in a curious sort of way, be also expressive of joy: the joy and thankfulness for all we had together, the thankfulness for all my present blessings .... All such powerful emotions that have the one outcome ....

Betty's document about undertaking her O.U. course has brought into more frontal consciousness for me, the idea that there is a sort of 'NOW' for me too at the present moment. I have been vaguely aware that my changed circumstances have made all sorts of things possible that were not before. I could have another ten years of reasonably effective functioning. How do I want to use that time? Who do I want to be? I have been consciously struggling to free myself from my academic work for some time, but I always seem to get dragged back into it. It was quite a victory to have successfully resisted the invitation to go to this year's international conference. I have really been trying to retire gracefully from my academic work ever since I had my stroke and gave up teaching . I could do so with a good conscience since I have written up and published all my extant research. I think I have done my bit.

I have been thinking that one tends to divide one's time into primary time and secondary time. Primary time is what the greater part of one's time and attention goes to, secondary time is the rest. One tends to spend one's primary time on what keeps body and soul together, or (as in the case of a home-maker) on what keeps other people's bodies and souls together. Of course, the ratio of primary to secondary time varies, both between different people, and at different times in a single person's life. What do I now want to spend my primary time on? I no longer have to earn my keep, as pensions and savings look after that, although I have to spend more time than formerly on the physical business of keeping body and soul together in the form of cooking, cleaning, housekeeping and such-like things; nevertheless, I still have a lot of primary time. To what do I want to devote my primary time? I have also, in recent years, been consciously fighting to be able to spend more time on drawing and painting. I also realise that I have been trying to get more time for listening to music. I have just seen that, if it was what I really wanted to do, I could devote my primary time to these artistic things. *Is* that what I want to do? I don't know yet – but at least I can now see that I have the freedom to do so if I wanted to. Just as the geological and academic hooks out of my past still drag at my garments, so also do those of the work ethic, in which primary time is supposed to go to something called 'work'. It is very difficult to detach those hooks; I tend to feel guilty if I am not spending major time on research and writing, and if I am not, the attitude of so many former colleagues tends to imply that I have less commitment to the subject than I should have. My life since I left school could be divided into blocks where my primary time was devoted to different things: four years getting degrees; eight years teaching and research overseas; seventeen years in 'education' and 'family' in England; twelve years full-time research and teaching, overseas again; eighteen years part-time research and writing, and looking after Betty. How should the last 'block' of my life be characterised? Perhaps I should do what Betty did – set out my 'problems' and my 'interests' and see what that comes up with.

Thomas Hunt has been in town for a week, and today I gave him lunch. I checked out beforehand whether I had received any sort of letter after Betty's death, but found that I had had none from either Thomas or his wife. I thought perhaps they had heard about it very late, and then thought it was too late to write; I knew I wrote informing most of our overseas friends who would be unlikely to hear in any other way, but I no longer had the list; I remember getting very tired at writing to such a large number of people, so thought perhaps I had flagged when it came to writing to the Hunts. But no, when we met, Thomas very quickly said there were two communications which he apologised for not answering; one was my Christmas card, and the other the note letting them know about Betty's death. The usual excuses about the busyness of university life were offered, which *could* wash as far as Thomas goes, but for his wife? I had always thought of her as a real friend to both of us, not only from the amount I had seen of her overseas, but also from her later contacts with Betty. But no, Betty's death had not ranked a letter from either of them – and for the rest of my two hours conversation with Thomas, Betty's death might not have occurred. I was flabbergasted, and hurt.

20 July 1994

I have been thinking about the piece Betty wrote, and the way she examined her problems and her interests as a preparation for finding a new identity and a new way of life – as it applies to me at the moment; because I have now come to such a moment for myself, being in a stage of transition; clearly in a transition from one way of life, with Betty, to – what? What are my problems? Well, the first is obviously this ongoing grief; then there is health, there is the continuing clinging hooks from my previous life, there is sex, there is ageing. What are my interests? My academic concerns, walking, Quakerism, drawing and painting, music.

23 July 1994

Last Saturday Pauline was knocked off her bike and broke her back. She is in hospital with a fractured vertebra and a great deal of pain. Fortunately so far they don't think there has been any damage to or pressure upon the spinal cord or the nervous system, which obviously is one's first anxiety. Everyone has to be patient and see how it goes, but that is not easy for anyone, least of all for Pauline.

Having had the great bundle of preoccupation over Betty for the last ten months, always in the forefront of my mind, always 'there', it is strange now to have another one, that of Pauline. It is like having a smaller supernova added to the original great blazing one.

Thinking again about my 'problems and interests':

Problems: the first is obviously this ongoing grief and adaptation to loss. It is still painful, and in a sense will always be there; but it is not, I feel, an 'insuperable problem'. I have had so much help from readings and from Virginia (although she says I have done a lot to help myself) that I can see now that there can be 'progress'; that although it is a fatuous cliché to say 'Time will heal the wound', nevertheless the passage of time is both necessary for, and allows, a kind of healing process to take place; the scar will always be there, but at any rate it is something if the open, running sore can, first, form a kind of scab over it. Although this scab can get knocked off several times, nevertheless another forms, perhaps smaller each time, until the last one comes off, leaving only the scar. I have faith that this can be so. The adaptation to loss and change is something associated with the grief, but is also something a bit different, which I think I have already said something about. For example, there are the obvious physical differences – such as doing all my own cooking and housekeeping; and one has to recognise that there are positive things about this as well as negative; although I have much that is new to learn, I only have to consult my own tastes, and can get and make for myself the things that I like! Of course the loss of companionship is the great thing; but then how incredibly lucky I am to have the children and grandchildren, and a host of friends. In addition, I have lived on my own before, and have considerable inner resources, so that I can enjoy the delights of solitude as well as enduring the pains of loneliness.

The next 'problem' I mentioned was 'health'. I had a stroke twelve years ago and for that reason have been told to take soluble aspirin every day to try and help prevent a recurrence. From time to time I get this annoying atrial fibrillation, which is painful and disabling but we now know is not life-threatening, although on two different occasions it has landed me with a week in the coronary care unit of the hospital. I would like to be able to avoid such attacks, but neither I nor my consultant can discover what the trigger is. I have an injured back, as a result of shifting heavy rocks some 45 years ago, and which has given me trouble ever since, sometimes very painful and badly disabling. I have therefore been very lucky to find an osteopath who has wrought something of a miracle on me. There is associated arthritis; fifteen years ago I had to give up playing the piano because of arthritic finger joints. My hearing is deteriorating and is a great trial.

'The continuing clinging hooks from my previous life'. When I am still asked to do things, to write things, or to lecture, and told that there is no one else who can do it as well, the flattery to my ego tends to make me ambivalent about saying 'No' unless I am very clear-sighted and firm. But I definitely do not want to be one of those aged academics who continue after they are past it, because this is supposed to show their dedication to the subject! Another reason for detaching these hooks from my past is that, knowing that I am not *au courant* with all the recent developments, I have lost my self-confidence. Therefore I have lost my former enjoyment of creative work in this field; therefore it is better not to make pathetic attempts 'to keep up'.

Of course the foregoing is one of the problems of ageing, which obviously are many. These problems are very much interwoven with health problems. Some time ago I described my body as being like a veteran car, in which you do not know which bit is going to be the next one to fail you or to drop off! The skill is in keeping the old banger on the road in spite of this. I get more easily and more quickly tired. I get more breathless walking uphill. I am told there are compensations for ageing, some of which I am not very vividly aware of. One good one, however, is that there is no longer a continual need to be hurrying; even this, however, does not come automatically, and is something which it is sense to teach myself in order to take advantage of the opportunity. I cannot walk as well as I used to, but have been trying to 'get it up again', especially as my osteopath encourages me to do long walks. Of course all these 'problems' interact and sometimes reinforce and complicate each other, some more than others. They also carry a lot of uncertainties, especially those of health; but it is no good worrying about that, one can just be thankful for every day that the problems do not unduly disturb one or interfere with planned activities.

Now as to 'interests'. These have changed in recent years, or been 'resumed'. My passion for my academic subject can no longer be actively pursued, at any rate in the form of it in which I have been most interested and in which I think I have made most contribution; and I have a distaste for trying to do something in a half-cock sort of way. I might possibly get interested in some sort of library research project, but at the moment I am doubtful about that. Before embarking on such a thing I would need to be able to see a lot of time available for it over a period of a good many months – and at the moment I can see no prospect of having to look for something 'to fill my time'.

Betty mentioned that she had been badly educated, and that she might in later life have an opportunity to remedy that. I was badly educated in the field of the visual arts, and perhaps now I have an opportunity to remedy that, because it is something that is so important in life for expression and communication, as well as a source of pleasure, if you know how to derive it. I obtained enormous pleasure from two absorbing days in Derbyshire on my course – but I have been so busy with other things since, that I have not yet succeeded in pursuing that further. I certainly mean to try. My grandfather's beautiful pen-and-ink sketches are an inspiration here. Why is it that there is such a widespread and ancient desire to 'capture' the three-dimensional visible world on a two-dimensional surface by making marks on a piece of paper or some other flat material? I want to organise my life so that I regularly get more time for that. This will be after I have completed dealing with Betty's things, moved into her room, and got a desk/table in there on which I can leave my art things out, and do not for ever have to swap over with word-processor and 'business' things on my present desk, as hitherto.

One of the difficulties of creating a new life and a new identity for oneself is that one's former colleagues and associates unwittingly try to cage you in your old one. They say to me 'What are you doing now?' mostly meaning 'What academic project are you now engaged in?' or 'What topic are you now writing on?' Alternatively, 'What new interest or occupation have you now taken up?', ready to pronounce approval or disapproval of that! Some have actually urged me to write an autobiography; I can envisage getting quite hooked on that, but I am in no hurry to begin. In fact, of course, in this particular piece I am writing an autobiography of the ten months since Betty died; possibly it should be rounded off at twelve months.

However I do eventually organise my life and its priorities, I can see I shall need to have an answer to the question 'What are you doing now?' which I can give with conviction and not in a defensive manner. It must be spoken of in a positive manner, as an opportunity to do something new, not as making the best of a bad job and preserving as well as possible the worn-out remnants of an old life. 'What are you doing now?' 'All the things which I'm interested in and wanted to do but not before had time to do.' This also fits in with what the best writers on bereavement have said about its being an opportunity for growth; maybe I am at last ready to contemplate that now, whereas hitherto most of my emotional energy has gone into coping with the pain. I can keep this idea of growth in my mind, although it is not something I would speak about to other people.

I am very interested in Quakerism, and hope I may be able to learn more about it and contribute more to my Meeting. I have already agreed to become an Overseer, the only new thing I have taken on since Betty died. (Two days ago I was asked to stand for the County Council, and had very little difficulty in saying No!). I have wanted to do a course at Woodbrooke for some time, and shall now do so when I can find the right one in the right slot of time – perhaps next autumn or winter.

Music is already coming back into my life, and is beginning to be a joy. No good contemplating playing the piano again because of arthritic fingers; should I return to playing the recorder, as I did forty years ago? I am already beginning to get music a bit better organised, with two radio cassette players, Radio 3 and Classic FM, and a number of tapes. There are two sorts of listening: 'real listening', when you give yourself to it entirely, and 'pleasant background'. I have also been to the opera four times in the last six months, and a number of concerts.

My other interest is walking, and it is encouraged for health reasons as well. Physical limitations are increasing with age, of course. I enjoy best 'a day out walking', perhaps with a pub lunch in the middle; I prefer walking on my own rather than in a party as I can go at my own pace. Better even than a day out walking, is several days in succession with bed-and-breakfast in between, in a long-distance walk. But ageing limbs and joints and muscles mean that I can only do that nowadays if I am in good training, which means taking shorter (say 5 miles) walks more frequently. This in turn means getting used to the idea of spending half a day walking any day of the week, whereas my mind-set has been that those are days for 'work', Saturday is the day for walking! These are all *mental* adjustments that have to be made.

11 August 1994

Some days ago it came to me quite strongly that there were certain *advantages* in living alone: it gives you freedom to do things you might otherwise not be able to. Recognising this does not diminish the loss of Betty or the loss of the *advantages* of companionship; it is just realistic to acknowledge the situation of living on my own. Accepting that there can be gains in this gives one a 'guilty' feeling to start with, the idea that if I feel that way I can't be missing Betty as much as I 'ought' to, and in fact, as much as I do. Yet another contradictory and confusing feeling. Virginia added that another advantage of living on one's own was that you had more opportunity to live with your real feelings; I can see that, but it had not occurred to me before, put quite like that. I had been aware of the advantages from being alone of being able to make the grief noises without feeling inhibited.

At the beginning of last week I had the pleasure of Tony staying for a couple of nights, and suddenly realised that it was an opportunity to enlist his help in swapping the beds over, so that I could move into Betty's room and take advantage of that lovely window. I have known for a long time that eventually I should do that, but I have not been able to do so before. I realised that I had now just about finished going through Betty's personal things, which has occupied me over the last month or so, and that now was the moment. Great question whether Betty's longer bed would go where mine was; measuring suggested to me that it would just go. Susan said 'Not a hope'; Tony said 'Oh it will go easily!'. There was nothing for it but to try and see. In the event it went with the thickness of a piece of paper to spare! I am now enjoying waking up in the morning, pulling back the curtain, and looking out on the fields and trees. It is really quite a step moving into Betty's room, but having left it until now, it has not been too difficult. I have also assembled all Betty's crosses, and other personal things, and been giving them away to her special friends.

One great joy: I have now finished the bound version of the extracts from letters about Betty which took me some six months to complete. I think I have made a good job of it, and the gold tooling on the blue leather looks particularly good. Pauline seemed well enough in hospital to show it to her, and she enthused about it. I now have the pleasure in prospect of showing it to the other children. Virginia was equally enthusiastic, and understood how therapeutic it had been for me doing it. I did not plan it to be so, but it just happened that way. The extracts build up to a picture of a very vivid character, but Virginia understood that I was not making any beatifications or pedestals. 'No', she said, 'you have already been able to face and speak of the less likeable aspects of her character.' 'It is you who are using the euphemisms', I said, 'Not "less likeable" – rather the honest word is "nasty"'. 'I call that healthy progress' said Virginia, and we had a good laugh over it. More seriously, I made the point that if, as I hoped I was, I was gaining 'repossession' of Betty, it was the real, human Betty, whom I knew so well, not just a latterly-created plaster saint. Yet that did not detract from the Betty of whom so much appreciation is expressed in the letters written by her friends.

My continuing preoccupation over the last two-and-a-half weeks has been Pauline in hospital flat on her back. Thank God the spinal cord has not been affected and there is no paralysis, but she has had an extremely painful and trying time. She and somebody else asked if it was not rather hard for me visiting her in the hospital, triggering memories of Betty's last days there. The answer was that there was one such flashing moment, when I was sitting at the end of the ward and they were doing something for Pauline in the bed; but it was a momentary pang, and all that has not been as bad as it might have been: I was so concerned for Pauline and her pain and condition. She said that, lying there with the terrible pain in her back, she thought of her mother's continual back pain, and felt guilty that she had not been more imaginative and sympathetic towards that pain and disability. I comforted Pauline on this as well as I could, and next day told her how useless I was to be any comfort and support to Betty when she lost David M., and that it was only after suffering the bereavement of losing her that I had some inkling of how she must have felt when she lost David, and of how terribly lonely she must have been. At the time, I, of course, was the last person to be any use to her.

I have had a sense of Betty 'fading'. Whereas in a sense I recognised that this could be called 'progress' in the process of mourning, neverthe-less it made me sad and part of me did not want it to happen. I am glad I have two good recent photographs of her.

19 August 1994

As a result of sorting through Betty's books, getting the Quaker Meeting librarian to come and select what she thought would be useful for the library there, getting another lady to select what she would find useful for herself in directing retreats, I looked at the first numbers of David M.'s personal newsletter which he wrote every three months for the last ten years of his life, and which he sent out to about seventy friends. From it I realised that I had my breakdown only eight months after Betty had installed him in our house; I had never noticed the juxtaposition before. Juxtaposition in time there certainly was – whether a causal relationship is impossible to say; I'm not making the mistake of *post hoc, propter hoc*. I've never understood that breakdown, but maybe David's coming to live under our roof was the final strain in a whole lot of stress which had been accumulating for a number of years.

Someone who knew Betty very well and was very fond of her, asked to have a second look at the book of letters. When she came across the extract which used the word 'sweet' of Betty, she laughed and exclaimed that that was something Betty was not! She also made some remark about Betty always getting what she wanted. Betty had apparently consulted this friend about having David to live in our house and had asked her what she thought my reaction was likely to be.

24 August 1994

Had another talk with Virginia today, in which she raised the question of how long we should go on. She wasn't trying to push me off, but felt I was sufficiently 'better' for us to be able to look at that. I told her I had already been wondering when I ought to be 'weaned'. I said I thought the time was coming when I should show her these jottings, and hoped I would be able to pay her the compliment of doing so without doing any editing, because I trusted her sufficiently for me to feel able to do that.

I mentioned that I found myself thinking a lot about the first ten years of our marriage, when we were happily getting on with what had to be done side by side. 'It is good to think of the good times', she said. I repeated what I had already said about being so grateful that we had been given the last fifteen years, in which we had brought so many things together. I said 'I suppose the good times were the first ten years, and the last fifteen years: the difficult times were the twenty-five years in between'.

Virginia spoke about the difficulties of looking at the bad times – but said that this was necessary too. This made me tell her about the discovery that my breakdown was only eight months after Betty took David under our roof; she was astonished that I had not been aware of this timing before. 'Well, there were so many other strands, and strains – and

I transferred my anger onto my boss, and blamed it all on my working conditions.' 'There must have been enormous anger in you over David, but you could not express it.' 'Oh no', I said, 'I saw myself as the nice liberal husband, who did not regard his wife as his possession, and thought she should be allowed to do what she wanted to do.' 'So there was all that anger you felt towards Betty, humanly and naturally – but at the same time there was the love. No wonder that inner conflict tore you apart – enough to give anyone a breakdown.'

10 September 1994

I find less urgency now to write in this account; does that mean that I have less need to, and less need of the therapy it offers? Once again the confusion and the contradiction: I suppose in a sense it means 'progress' in the grieving process, and yet there is part of me that doesn't want to admit that I have less need of it. Anyway, I am coming up to the end of the first year, and although many people say 'It takes two years', I trust the second year is not worse than the first, like the second six months was worse than the first. It certainly does not feel as if the second year must be worse than the first, so I hope I can be allowed that! It's a very funny feeling, thinking that it was a year ago all this happened: in some ways I can't believe it was a year ago, it is still yesterday; and yet in another way it has been such a long, long year.

13 September 1994

In meeting for worship two days ago, I thought that I had been 'praying' for so many different people and for different members of the family, that I would treat myself to a bit of praying for myself! They say one should not forget this. It made me ask myself the question: 'Well, what do you really *want?*' – and I realised there were principally two things. The first was connected with the grieving process; I want to reach the point where I can feel comfortable with it; is that reasonable? Is what I am saying that every time I think (more than superficially) about Betty, I don't want to have the great drag it so often entails; or do I? Confusion and conflicting emotions again. I want to feel comfortable not only with myself, but also with myself in relation to other people; I think I am probably further on with that than with the first. I know that I take pleasure in talking about Betty naturally to other people whether they like it and are comfortable with it or not. I almost compel them to be natural and comfortable! However, I am prepared to go along with the idea that it takes two years to reach this point of feeling comfortable with it for myself. By this I don't mean that I shall then have 'got over the grief', the grief and the sense of loss will in a sense always be there, I think. But I can only describe what

I mean by using the word comfortable. Perhaps what I mean really is a total acceptance of it.

The second thing I want is to grow spiritually. I know this only comes from working at it (but not too hard!) and giving time to it. I probably ought to do more reading connected with it. I have toyed with the idea of spending a term at Woodbrooke, and I know exactly what I would want to do on that – acquainting myself with modern New Testament scholarship, and learning more about Quakerism. A little thing I know I can do for a start – and that is to read regularly and properly my copy of *The Friend*. It comes every week, but I do not give it sufficient priority for it to get properly read before the next one comes a week later! To read it intelligently I know I need to highlight the bits that strike me or I want to remember, but I have been inhibited from doing that because I pass my copies on to someone else; now I am not going to be inhibited by that, and if they do not like having a highlighted copy, they can lump it – or get their own; they might even be interested to see what it is that I do highlight!

16 September 1994

Yesterday I had a bad 'Betty day', full of nostalgia. What is nostalgia? Literally it means 'home-sickness'. I suppose that means a longing for the comfortable and the familiar. But of course it is extended to a sadness for what is gone and cannot be recaptured. This I find quite difficult now, and I find it so often in relation to Betty and the early years of our marriage. It was set off yesterday because, when I was driving to visit a former colleague, I happened to take a road where we used to take the children on picnics in the days when we had Nursie – a charming corner beside a stream; the stream was small enough and accessible enough for the children to be able to enjoy playing in it quite safely. I think there is the nostalgia itself, of past happy times, but also it underlines the present loss because had I driven past there with Betty we should have reminisced about those former happy days together, and now I have no one to share that with.

I drove on to have lunch with a former colleague and his wife who were associated with myself and Betty in the first five years of our marriage; this inevitably added to the nostalgia. Found myself half-groaning, half-shouting at it while driving home. I find this tends to happen driving the car, especially any distance, as driving does not occupy the whole of one's attention so the rest can be occupied by Betty; and also, being quite on my own, it doesn't matter how much noise I make or what I say or shout. The nostalgia was added to by a friend bringing me a piece she had written about Betty, once again with emphasis on those brave days when Betty and I were tackling life in harness together, she always with so much courage and élan.

BETTY

I see you with black hair, wearing blue
Bright with the thought of meeting your husband
After his weeks away.

I see you in a flowered blouse
Placing a red rose in a glass vase on his supper tray
Before joining a discussion group
In your drawing room.

I see you in a red jacket
Dashing to Brownies, the Red Cross, a church meeting
Heavily involved.

I see you in a pink nightie in the nursing home
Where bronchitis took you, and I
Closed curtains against the lightning
When we hated a storm together.

I see you in a summer dress in the orchard
Pouring tea and orange squash
Crying to the children with your haphazard efficiency
'No drinks on the rug!'

I see you in the white skirt, pleats swinging,
"So impractical" we said,
"But so good for the spirit this year".

I see you in a blue house coat
Saying 'I want lots of daffodils'
And after I had brought them, the house of death
Was full of flowers, and your faith.

I see you in ruby corduroy
So becoming, with the grey hair and grey dog beside you,
Essays and art books scattered now,
A new era.

Later – the walking frame, the adapted car,
The wheelchair,
Odd that I see none of those
Yet hear your voice.

Of course I realise that all this nostalgia may not be just 'Betty-loss', but that some of it is the nostalgia of an old man recalling his lost youth – *yet* I am not aware of having felt any of that outside the context of Betty. How can I turn the sadness of this nostalgia into the joy of knowing that we did have all that? I can do it intellectually, but do not seem able to emotionally.

Marriage between two individuals who give each other enough space and respect to be their own persons is incredibly difficult. It seems to be rarely attained. But if partnership and companionship of this kind can be achieved, the rewards are beyond rubies. Correspondingly, the loss by death of one partner in such a marriage is for the survivor of a magnitude beyond calculation. The extent of the loss is proportional to the treasures lost; the pain is proportional to the former pleasure; the amputation is proportional to the strength of the former attachment; the grief is proportional to the absent satisfaction and comfort. Will the growth of which Kübler-Ross speaks be proportional to the depth of the grief? How much will this mourning fertilise the soil where the dying seed falls? "Except a corn of wheat fall into the ground and die, it abideth alone; but if it die it bringeth forth much fruit" (John 12, 24). Was Jesus expressing the same sort of insight as Kübler-Ross?

22 September 1994

For the last five or six weeks I have been quite busy preparing for my day of keeping open house on the anniversary of Betty's death. (I cannot *believe* it is a year ago; it seems quite impossible.) I got the idea of giving all the kind people who had written things which I included in 'the Betty book' a chance to see it, so thought I would have it available throughout one Saturday, when they could come at whatever time suited them. So I'm keeping open house from 10 a.m. to 10 p.m. on that day, having the book available, and providing light refreshments. Initially I was only going to invite those who had contributions in the book, but it was I who had selected who those should be, and there were others who had written to me at the time; then it became difficult to draw the line between them and many others whom I did not want to be left out of such a celebration of Betty's life. Some of them were overseas, and although there was no hope of their coming, I did not want them omitted; so the numbers grew to nearly 300 invitations, including family, Quakers and all.

When a friend called the other day, to my surprise she said: 'I think you ought to get re-married'. Such an idea came as a considerable shock, because such an idea seems so far from my thoughts. I said: 'Oh no, I don't think I've still got the energy for all that give-and-take.' 'Oh no', she said, 'it doesn't have to be like that. You want to find someone who would *like* looking after you – there are some people like that.' Well, she may be right, but it would obviously have to be the right person, who did feel like that; but it sounds rather like a one-sided sort of marriage. What would 'she' get out of it? Another consideration concerning marrying again would be the children's reaction, both to the fact of it, and to the person concerned; there would also be legal complications if I married again, in relation to the children, my will, housing, and suchlike practical affairs. Marriage as such is as much a legal matter as one of relationship. The logic of that would be to find someone who would be willing to live with me and 'look after' me without getting married. How fair would that be?

And then of course, in the middle of my lunch, I had a weep, a good sobbing weep – which I don't think I have had for over a month. Once again, triggered by music; in this case one of Vila-Lobos's Bachianas Brazilianas, 'The Little Train of the Chapparal' – which is a *fun* thing, with a joyous, happy theme – but the last time I heard it was when Betty and I played our LP of it together, before all the LP's had to go in the house-move. Anyway it set me weeping, and being by myself, I made no attempt to control it. Before that was finished, Pauline rang, asking me to identify a piece of music she played over the phone on a tape, because she said she thought I used to play it, about which she was right; it was a Chopin Nocturne. So naturally, after I'd finished talking to Pauline, the weeping started all over again ... Although the need for weeping may be less now, and less frequent, I think it is as if it builds up beneath the surface of ordinary living and ordinary behaving – and then something, like a piece of music, takes the lid off ...

A reflection has just come to me, that if anyone should ever read all this, they should not feel sorry for me! Sympathetic, yes, but that is subtly different. Sorrows, losses, sufferings, griefs – these are part and parcel of life, and I imagine there are none who are immune from these 'slings and arrows of outrageous fortune', and it is surely right to feel sympathy for those who endure them. But does anyone need to be sorry for my shouts and tears and groans and cries? Loving sympathy, yes, so comforting – but there should be no trace of pity. We have to cope with these griefs – and tears and groans are the natural means we are given to help us cope with them; rather we should be sorry for those who *cannot* weep. What a wonderful prayer Yvonne Cornwall uttered for me when she wrote: 'May you have the gift of tears.'

29 September 1994

Today I met Sharon, whose husband died a month or so after Betty. I made no bones about asking her how she was getting on; initially she answered that purely on the surface and material level, about tidying

Michael's things, disposing of his books and papers etc. Later we spoke of the more emotional level of reaction, and I felt she did not understand some of the things I was talking about; she seemed to think it extraordinary that she found herself in floods of tears in bed one night – and spoke of this as if it were a unique occasion. She gave me the impression that 'her grief was not as bad as mine'. But how can you ever really tell? She was Michael's second wife, but had been married to him for about 30 years.

The last few days I have been waking up with that terrible depression again; feeling so dull and flat; perhaps not as bad as six months ago, but pretty leaden even so. I would like that 'to get better' but wonder if it will, or whether it will be an endemic condition, breaking out at intervals. Rachmaninov's 'Rhapsody on a theme of Paganini' triggered me off weeping again. That was the natural uninhibited reaction; but I am wondering whether, having now had a year's weeps, I should begin to be warned by the pricking behind my eyes and attempt to resist the development into weeping. I can't *believe* it is a year since Betty died.

CHAPTER 4

The Second Year

2 October 1994

L AST FRIDAY SUSAN GAVE me marvellous help getting ready for
Betty's 'Celebration' next day, bringing over all the food and other
things we had bought together for the purpose the previous Wednesday,
helping me fetch the wine and glasses, arranging the furniture, doing the
flowers I had bought etc. On the Saturday, i.e. yesterday, I got up early
so as to have time to do all the jobs I needed to do, which was a good
thing because Richard rang up to say he would not be able to be with me
at 9 o'clock because of a hitch, but he would be there by 9.30 or soon
after, because he knew the first guest was coming at 10.00. The 'hitch'
was that his wife had fallen downstairs on Thursday morning, fortunately
not broken anything, but was very immobile, and needed help even to get
in and out of bed. So it was very good of Richard to come at all, and he
was a marvellous help – as were all the children, bless them, who had
arranged a rota of about three hours each with half-an-hour overlap, so
that Richard was succeeded by Pauline, Susan and Tony in that order,
the latter arriving about 6.30 for the rest of the day, and staying the night.
I had the Betty book available on the desk in the study/spare room for
people to see, invited the first comers to go and look at it at once before
they had food and drink, but most of the rest had their turn after they had
had their refreshments. I was very fierce with them about not taking any
food and drink into that room, just in case of accidents. They were all
very appreciative of the book, some quite ecstatically so. I think those who
had really known Betty were very pleased to see such a collection of
tributes to her.

About 120 people came during the course of the twelve hours, and
fortunately, having asked them to say approximately what time they were
coming, I was able to stagger them so that there was no terrible conges-
tion at any one time, although of course there were peaks and troughs of
numbers. (Some turned up without ever having answered the invitation!)
So the arrangements all seemed to work smoothly, thanks to having kept

the refreshments fairly simple and to the marvellous help from the children – and some of the grandchildren, who also got stuck in with things like washing up. I did get very tired with so much standing around, but the children, again, were very good in making me sit down from time to time, and I got a second wind after about 5 o'clock. No less than sixteen people brought bunches and bouquets of flowers, so that the house is now an absolute bower. A former colleague and his wife drove all the way from Birmingham. So many people said they had really enjoyed it, and they really seemed to mean it. I myself enjoyed it greatly, much more than I had anticipated, people were so kind. At the end of the day I felt it had been a very happy one. One nice thing said was: 'I hope Betty is aware of all this in some way; she would have been tickled pink'. I was indeed very tired at the end of it, so after Tony and I had done a bit of clearing up and clearing away, I went and had a lovely soak in a hot bath – and went to bed feeling content.

I think maybe it was quite a good thing for me to have this definite marker of twelve months since Betty died; there's not much point in some 'anniversaries', but on this occasion I think it worked. I wanted it to be a happy day, and it was. I know one cannot go by the timetable and the calendar, but I feel I can now say: 'Well, I've done the first year.' I may even be on an even keel – and yet part of me still doesn't feel like that. To think that I had been congratulating myself that I was now emotionally more balanced! Still so much I don't understand. Once again, I suppose 'acceptance' is the key word; a curious thing is that I think I can feel the beginnings of some peace coming. I had formulated the thought only three days ago that I was still very much without it.

3 October 1994

I'm astonished at how much 'lighter' I feel today. Why should I feel so much 'better' just because the artificial time interval of a year has gone by? What magic is there in that? Of course I think it has been helped by the success of Saturday's celebration, the nice things people said, the wonderful bower of flowers I now have all over the flat. Today I now feel so much more *able to enjoy* the many blessings I have. I knew I had them before and could give thanks for them, but I think at the moment I can actually enjoy them more. Sitting out in the sunshine on the patio contributes! I think also, possibly, that hitherto I have been reluctant to 'let Betty go'; now perhaps I am beginning to be able to. Also, somehow, it seems more possible to be forward-looking.

This more forward-looking means that I should look at my life and consider carefully how I want it to be. I have so many different interests, as well as people asking me to do things, that it would be very easy to fritter my time away on a too-great diffuseness of effort – particularly as ageing means that total effort and energy are now less. I am beginning to learn to say 'No', but perhaps I need to develop this more; and part of the solution may lie in not trying to do all the different things concurrently, but in having concentrations on different ones in succession – some lend themselves to this sort of treatment, some do not. I have also just discovered the value of keeping whole days free, so that they are available for walking, for painting and drawing, for writing etc. When someone wants to see me, I have tended to look in my diary and choose a day when I've got nothing else on – so that then there *is* something on that day, and bang goes a clear day; better to fit in two or three engagements when people want to see me on the same day, and leave more days free for what *I* want to do!

Music still has the power to 'set me off', i.e. trigger the tears which are still not far below the surface, although not usually nowadays leading to the attacks of deep sobbing I was formerly subject to. This morning it was Pachelbel's 'Canon' which did it; yesterday it was the General Thanksgiving from the 1666 English Prayer Book, which someone recited at a Thanksgiving meeting for Anne C.; it is one of the most beautiful ordering of words in the English language, as well as being a very powerful prayer; and of course for me it has such nostalgic overtones of my upbringing in the Anglican church. At Anne's Thanksgiving Meeting I fear I found myself thinking more of Betty than of Anne!

25 October 1994

I've just been away for a week with Tony and his family, to use it as a base for doing some walking. Well, that's one thing that has been decided for me! On our first walk, after the first seven miles I had one of my heart fibrillation attacks, with severe chest pain, so after two hours rest on the grass in a churchyard, I had to make my way back to the car by the shortest route; rested the next two days and then tried again – only to have the form of attack I've had before, after I got home, of passing out and vomiting. So I reckon I'm not meant to do as much walking as I have been doing; annoying, as I've done lots of long walks in the last five months without ill effects. Had three more heart 'incidents' after getting home. But at any rate it may settle one of the priorities of how I spend my time, which I was discussing above: perhaps less time for walking now, at any rate long-distance walking.

While I was away, I had some quiet thinking time when I was forced to rest, and came up with the following. I think I am making a new psychic space for Betty, different from the one she was in for me when she was alive. Is this the 'repossession' of her, of which Joanna spoke? Even though it has taken much longer to make this psychic space for Betty than Joanna spoke of. Maybe it was only possible to start building this space when I had achieved acceptance of her death.

I can conceive that this space could be filled with joy.

I think I am probably being selective in what I am putting into this new psychic space – I am tending to put there the glad and happy and positive memories rather than the sad and bitter and negative. I think I can be allowed to do this *now* – because I know I am doing it, it is not false, I am not creating an unreal saint, and because I *have* now faced the memories of the less positive, less likeable aspects of Betty. Perhaps this is an *opportunity* which bereavement offers – in this new psychic space to populate it with the happy memories rather than the unhappy without being false or hypocritical about the latter.

It was ironical that on my return from Tony's I found awaiting me a request from a former colleague for a complicated and urgent reference for a job application, and I had only been in the house a few hours when I had telephone calls asking me to sort out a tricky matter with a member of my Quaker Meeting, and from the science correspondent of a national newspaper wanting a whole lot of detailed information for a book review. Why can't I just say 'NO', No, No, No! to these requests? I tell myself that I only haven't said 'No' because the Quaker one is important, the reference affects someone's career, and the one about the book will only get what attention I can give it in the next two days.

31 October 1994

I mentioned to Helen that I was going down to Kelmscott Manor the next day, and in view of Betty's interest in William Morris said how much I wished I could be taking Betty with me. She said: '*Take* her with you!' – and I did. Helen also said, in another part of the conversation: 'Betty is happy now: she is happy, happy, *happy!*' She said it with such a wonderful conviction, I was glad to be reminded of this, and it recalled my vision of her a year ago as 'a ball of joy'.

In the fourth stage of grief we are bidden to 'Say goodbye and build a new life'. I would give a new meaning to the 'saying goodbye', as for me it is not saying farewell for ever, but only saying goodbye to that Betty who lived with me for fifty-three years; and part of that process is saying *welcome* to the new Betty who can be with me now, the one who occupies the new psychic space I have made for her. Perhaps this is the bit Judy Tatelbaum meant when she described it as 'Letting go of your attachment both to the deceased and to sorrow', which I so fought against when I first encountered it ten months ago. I would still word it a bit differently:

'letting go of your sorrow', yes; but in place of 'letting go of the deceased', I would rather put 'transforming the deceased'.

I think I *am* 're-investing in life' now, thirteen months on, which is said to be necessary, although so difficult, after severe bereavement, if one is to 'give some meaning to the person's death.' I did not really understand that when I first read it eight months ago, and I am not sure that I do now, but maybe it is what has resulted in making the new psychic space for Betty. Dare I also hope that, having been emotionally knocked off balance for so long, that I am now beginning to recover a bit more balance?

9 November 1994

Maybe I really am beginning to get more emotional balance again, things certainly do seem different. I weep much less, less frequently, and less violently when it does happen. "The Lady of Shallott" triggered the tears into my eyes again two evenings ago when I happened to read it again, after I had got the Tennyson out because at a meeting that evening someone had quoted 'Lest one good idea corrupt the world' and I was sure that was a misquotation – which it is:

> 'The old order changeth, yielding place to new,
> And God fulfils himself in many ways,
> Lest one good custom should corrupt the world.'

The Lady of Shallott did not trigger me because I identified Betty with the Lady of Shallott, which I never have, but just because it is such a movingly beautiful poem.

It seems strange that the move into the second year should make such a difference. Am I really at last beginning 'to let Betty go?' To be repossessing her? To be some way further on to 'completing my grief?'

18 November 1994

It is certainly 'different' now – sometimes 'better', sometimes a bit as if I am 'harder' now, less feeling – is this a different way of saying that I have achieved more emotional balance? A bit 'low' sometimes, but nothing like the depression of six months ago. I suppose it is all part of the transition into a new stage. Even Brahms Symphony No 3 did not produce a tear!

20 November 1994

I feel strangely unpeaceful. Having sensed myself to be so much 'better' once the twelve months was over, and having achieved some peace, I seem to have taken a backward step. I wonder why. Perhaps just the rhythm of the way it has to go. When it was at its worst, I used to feel as if great waves of pain and grief were breaking over me. Well, it is not like that now, but I seem to be experiencing a great wave of *missing*, just missing Betty; and feeling very acutely aware of her. Is she conveying something, is this feeling independent of me but being conveyed to me? There is something very, very definite about it. Is she in fact trying to give me some peace? I spoke too soon about being dry-eyed in the presence of music – pride always comes before a fall. Just before having lunch with my brother Alec today I was listening on the car radio to Desert Island Discs, and in the first place who should be the castaway but Joan Baez, and what should the recording be that she chose but Kathleen Ferrier singing Handel's 'Those that bring good tidings' from Judas Maccabaeus? I had to sit in the car for five minutes while I pulled myself together before I could go in to lunch. Oh these waves of emotion! How one wishes one could be on an even keel – and yet part of me still doesn't. To think that I had been congratulating myself that I was now emotionally more balanced! Still so much I don't understand. Once again, I suppose 'acceptance' is the key word; I have to learn to accept the strange bit that is now.

21 November 1994

Thought a lot yesterday about *why* this feeling of unpeacefulness, of being 'low' should be hitting me just now. I wondered whether it was because I have put myself under pressure to get my present bit of writing finished. I know that recently I have not been so good at coping with pressures and dead-lines as I used to be – formerly such dead-lines were just part of my stock-in-trade; Betty once said she thought I worked better under pressure – now it fusses me more; I suppose this is one of the effects of ageing. So nowadays I feel better without time-lines and pressures; therefore it is up to me to avoid them. Therefore I have been saying to myself: 'It doesn't *matter* if you don't get it done for the deadline.'

I have just looked at that lovely photograph of Betty which I took two or three years ago and have hanging above my desk, and found myself saying to her spontaneously, thinking about our life together: 'Oh, darling, it was glorious!' – and then, with an adjunct of honesty – 'At least, bits were glorious. We had a lot that was glorious!'

2 December 1994

For the last two or three weeks I have been feeling increasingly depressed, and increasingly unsettled. I thought I was supposed to be 'over' these manifestations of bereavement! But I have to admit that that is how it has been.

About five weeks ago I had five of my heart fibrillation 'incidents' in a fortnight, after only having had one or two in the previous six months. As a result of this the medics have put me on beta-blockers for the last four weeks and today I had to see my G.P. about their renewal. The question came up about side-effects from these drugs, and I mentioned the depression; the doctor did not think this could be laid at the door of the beta-blockers. This led her to suggest that I should resume writing my diary, which I thought I had brought to a conclusion some weeks ago. So this is what I am now doing. In the course of this conversation she said 'You can tell yourself to do things, can't you, but it is nicer when you have someone to tell you to do them, isn't it?'

One irritating thing at the present moment: because we have been having unseasonably sunny weather and I have been taking advantage of it, people have been saying to me, usually with a note of surprise in their voice: 'You're looking very well!', and one can detect something of a note of relief in their voices, implying that they are glad that I am doing well in 'getting over' my bereavement. When this comes at one when one is feeling absolutely lousy, and as depressed as hell, it is very annoying. I want to scream at them that the feeling inside is exactly the opposite of 'well' – but it doesn't seem quite right to do so. I even get it on the telephone, if I answer somebody in a reasonably lively way: 'How are you? You sound splendid!' The next time somebody does that to me, I shall probably say something very rude; and then regret it. Oh Hell!

6 December 1994

Ageing and bereavement coming together adds to the confusion. How much is the depression and unsettled feeling the result of one or the other or a mixture of both? The whole situation exacerbated by pranging my car. There was not only the shock of the actual accident (although nobody hurt, thank God), but also the anger and disappointment at myself because it has to be partly my fault. I was gauging the gap between a car parked on the left of the road and an oncoming furniture van travelling very fast. A car from behind the parked car suddenly pulled out into the middle of the road and stopped there, right in front of me. My eyes were on the approaching furniture van and did not see the car pulled into the middle of the road in time. I slammed on my brakes but hit the stationary car at about 10 m.p.h. – not enough to hurt anybody but enough to do a lot of damage to the cars, including puncturing my radiator. I ought to have seen the manoeuvre of the car in front sooner than I did. Followed all the business of exchanging names and addresses, getting the car to the garage, insurance etc., etc., but worse than being without a car is the loss of self-confidence – such a feature of bereavement anyway. I could have done without this.

I asked the doctor whether the beta-blockers could slow down one's reaction time, but of course she said no – and pointed out that reaction time did increase with increasing years – which I knew already but which was the last thing I wanted to hear. So that's one more thing, in addition to the heart trouble, I have to attribute to ageing and my physical condition, along with getting so clumsy and nearly knocking myself out when I recently walked head first into the glass panel of the shut patio window-door, when I thought it was open.

I had a bit of a moan to Helen about it all, how much I *hated* all these manifestations of ageing but supposed it was something on which I had to stick a label of 'Acceptance'. She agreed, and pointed out how much she and Betty had had to do just that with their increasing physical infirmities; they used to encourage and support each other in the process. I am not good at such acceptance. I have been accustomed to being tough and self-reliant; now I have to accept that I no longer am to the extent that I was. No wonder that I feel depressed and unsettled about it. Having at last reached a measure of 'acceptance' over Betty's death, I now have this other thing to cope with – without her to moan to about it! I'm not really sorry for myself, because I have so many blessings, but the adjustments take time. Some of the writings on bereavement I have read have pointed out that *any* big loss can carry some of the features of bereavement; I am now experiencing the slow loss of my self-reliance and self-confidence. It underlines what the progressive loss of her independence must have meant to Betty. I realised it to a considerable extent at the time, but not, I think, with the empathy I have now.

Oddly enough, I have a numb feeling over Betty at the moment – which is what one is supposed to have at the time of the bereavement, not fourteen months later! Is it that, a real numb feeling, or that I am beginning to hold her in that new psychic space I have created for her? Is it the 'letting go' or the 'repossession' people speak of?

7 December 1994

Still confused whether my present feeling low is the current stage of my bereavement, or depression at the manifestations of old age. I spoke about the need for the *acceptance* of old age, but I guess that before that can come there is need for its *recognition*: that the clumsiness, the forgetting, the stumbling, the heart trouble, the inability to do long-distance walks, the tiredness, the increasing deafness, the poorer sight, the car crash – all these *are* old age. I have to recognise: *I am old*. There! I have said it. It was as hard to do so as to say 'Betty is dead'. In other words there is the same kind of *disbelief* that old age has really come upon me as there was over Betty's death. In both cases there can be intellectual recognition and belief, but an emotional recognition and belief comes more slowly and with greater difficulty. There is a diabolical combination: the tiredness of ageing and the exhaustion of grieving, sometimes resulting in a freezing rigidity of the limbs (Mary Stott: 'I could barely lift my hand from the arm of a chair.')

An extraordinary thing yesterday evening, when I was talking to one of my Oversight group. He had come to Betty's anniversary celebration, but when I looked round for him found that he had slipped away without a word. So he asked to look again at the book of extracts about her. This led to conversation about her, and in particular to the subject of the tea-party at the Meeting House after the funeral. He said that on that occasion he 'saw' Betty flitting around to this one and that one like a good fairy, touching each on the shoulder with her wand and giving a wish or something good. He said he always used to see 'the impish, gamine quality' in Betty, 'like a real Tinkerbell'. I told him how extraordinary this was because that was my pet name for her from the time we were engaged; it became shortened to 'Tink' (of which the children were aware, and for whom it was the occasion of teasing us). Of course he had only known Betty in her physically disabled state, during the last six years or so. He said that the gift which Betty gave him at the funeral tea-party was the meeting and conversation with Helen whom he found amazingly intuitive in knowing 'where he was'.

27 December 1994

Quite a lot has happened since I last wrote in this diary. I went away for my ten days art course in Derbyshire, and the technical side of that was as good as always, except that the increased numbers meant that we were very crowded; but the depression followed me there and was very bad indeed. I found it a tremendous effort to be at all 'decent' to the people on other courses, and to engage in social chat and intercourse; I either had to force myself to do it, or just didn't bother and relapsed into silence. (Mary Stott's 'Creeping paralysis of the social responses.') I think I am suffering from an increased level of my undifferentiated anxiety. But what am I afraid of? Of behaving like an old man does, of doing stupid things, of making a fool of myself, of being unreliable, of being unable to cope with what is involved in living for me now. I *have* accepted some of the things – the not walking, letting Richard drive me to and from Derbyshire etc., but I need to accept them all. I must try to develop the same kind of attitude as in the loss of Betty: 'The Lord gave, the Lord hath taken away. Blessed be the name of the Lord.' Such acceptance is not resignation, it is a recognition of old age and a *cooperation* with it. Maybe that's what Betty meant in her prayer when she spoke of 'lovingly accepting' her disabilities. The Lord gave me physical and mental strength; he is now progressively removing them. It is natural that such loss brings great distress, as any loss does. I have wondered whether these losses would be easier to bear if they were sudden – but I do not think so; given the choice, I would not choose to have another stroke! In addition, somewhere I have read that the gradual failure of powers is a merciful preparation for death; perhaps that is true.

On the phone I told Helen how depressed I had been, but felt that I ought not to be. She almost yelled reproof down the phone: '*Ought* not to be? What do you mean? Don't you realise you are still *grieving*? You've still got a lot to do.'

Quite unexpectedly, when I woke up on my first morning at home again, the depression had miraculously lifted; it was wonderful, and it has stayed that way – although the near-exhilaration of the depression going naturally cannot remain at such a high level. Whether it was due to no longer having to make social efforts, as in Derbyshire, or whether it was getting my car back with no fuss from the insurance people and finding that I was reasonably confident driving again – I do not know. Whatever the reason I am grateful.

When I visited Helen and we were talking about anger, she evidently thought I was strong enough to take the information that Betty was often angry with me. 'Not for any misdemeanour', she said, 'but she used to say "How can I be angry with him when he is so good to me and does so much for me? But so often he won't let me do things *for myself*; he takes away my independence." I thought I had learnt to be well aware of this problem, which I know I did have to learn and I don't know at what stage of Betty's increasing disability Helen was speaking. The other side of the coin was that I sometimes accused Betty of being ungracious about what I tried to do for her, going so far once as actually to use that word. 'It is more difficult to receive than to give'. Part of the pathos of the situation of a disabled person and their carer. Helen said that Betty also complained that sometimes I was thoughtless. I dare say. That conversation made me pretty wet-eyed again, the first time for a couple of months. Helen suggested that perhaps I had still not yet wept enough.

Mary Stott speaks of the look on the faces of those having suffered loss, whether the bereaved or those having lost their jobs.

'I was working on the *Leicester Mail* and can remember some of the refugees from Fleet Street turning up there. I didn't recognise their lost look then. You have to have been bereaved yourself to recognise the face of bereavement. Artists and sculptors portray it as an anguished cry, but it has a bewildered, zombie face. I know now.'

So do I. A bewildered zombie is often how I feel.

28 December 1994

Saw Virginia again, as recommended by my G.P. when I was so depressed. Said I felt a bit of a fraud, now I felt 'better'. Virginia emphasised that fourteen months was still *comparatively* early days. She understood, too, about the confusions of bereavement and ageing being mixed up. She agreed how maddening it was, in the ageing process, when you complained of something to a medic, that they simply said 'Well, you know, you must expect this kind of thing at your age!' 'Yes', she said, 'you *know* that, but you want the medics to do something to make it *better!*' To say: 'You must expect it at your age' is *no* help to the one ageing, it is merely of comfort to the medics as absolving them from further diagnosis or treatment. If someone tries to soften the sufferings of old age by calling it 'Anno Domini' I want to scream. My dear G.P. did very much better on one occasion, when I was asking her what could be triggering my bouts of heart arrhythmia, she hesitated, looked at me and said: 'Well, you know, your heart is as old as you are!'

I was able to agree with Virginia that even if the bereavement situation was not 'better', it was very definitely different. I characterised it as a move from the grinding misery of a year ago to what I would describe as just sadness – with continuing "missing".

3 January 1995

Ever since I first realised that, if rightly used, the 'life after' was an opportunity to grow, a chance to learn, I have wondered what the special lesson was for me – because obviously it is not the same for everybody: people are different, and bereavement may hit them at different points in their spiritual pilgrimage.

I think what I have been painfully learning is that loss can be used positively; that it is not a matter of acquiescence or resignation, but an acceptance that is welcoming. I tried, fumblingly, to explain that idea to someone I thought might understand and she seemed to think that that was impossibly hard, something only for saints. Nevertheless, it is the idea I am trying to feel my way towards. 'To rejoice at one's pains' certainly seems the superhuman masochistic attainment of saints only. But it is only masochistic and unhealthy if the pains are self-inflicted (like self-flagellation). But to embrace the suffering when it comes to you from outside .... that surely is different. If one comes to the idea that joy *can* triumph over suffering I think it can begin as just a sort of dogged faith – and then one can be 'surprised by joy'.

The disabilities of ageing hit me harder than I realised or would allow, and made me very depressed. Now I can see that it would be possible to embrace them positively and *actually be grateful for them*. That looks like a heroic achievement. But the trick is to remember that one would not be feeling the pains of ageing if one had not known the joys and the delights and the pleasures of youth and maturity. So that when one is giving thanks for the ageing, one is not only giving thanks for having *survived* to old age (with each new day as a bonus), but also for all that one has had leading up to it.

I found a wonderful expression of this idea in Yeats:

> An aged man is but a paltry thing
> A tattered coat upon a stick, unless
> Soul clap its hands and sing, and louder sing
> For every tatter of its mortal dress.

So maybe this is the lesson I can learn out of the 'growth opportunity' I have been given.

There *is* joy in this discovery. I clap my hands and sing.

11 January 1995

An extraordinary thing happened to me a week or two ago. I had heard that the parents of the warden of a nearby Retirement Home, whom I knew, had both died within a short space of time of each other. It so happened that a couple of days later I had to go to that building for a meeting of an organisation I had had nothing to do with before, and which I had some doubts about. When I arrived, there was the warden sitting in the foyer. I went straight up to her and said I had heard about her loss and that I was so sorry. We got talking about it, and after about a quarter of an hour she invited me up to the warden's flat – and we went on talking for about an hour and a half, until her husband came home. She was obviously very hard hit by her bereavement, and wanted to talk about it and about her parents. I had no compunction in cutting the meeting I had been going to, as I was obviously doing something much more useful. The warden wasn't sure whether I had been going to the meeting or whether I was going to see her, and it seemed inappropriate to enlighten her. Was it just coincidence that I had been going to the meeting of that organisation for the first time, just when the warden was in need of some love and comfort?

I think I am feeling – dare I say it? – a bit better. Self-confidence has been helped by small things – making an even more successful 'Queen

Mother's Cake', and, discovering for myself, when I had a bunch of green celery not nice for a salad, how to do it as a braised vegetable – and it was delicious.

Judith Viorst's *Necessary Losses* is excellent. A few quotations:

(Quoting Freud) 'We are never so defenceless against suffering as when we love, never so helplessly unhappy as when we have lost our loved object or its love.'

'It is our human fate to suffer, to greater or lesser degree, from the curse of ambivalence.' (Speaking of love/hate/envy in human relationships).

'Mourning is the process of adapting to the losses of our life.'

Yesterday morning sitting on the patio after breakfast, I set down the following lines:

> Our losses are our gains.
>
> When losses come
> We cannot see the gain
> For pain.
>
> Time, the refreshing river,
> Allows an opening of the eyes
> To see our losses as our gains –
> Once more the oneness realise.
>
> The losses last,
> The red-hot iron still sears the soul,
> The losses do not vanish in the past –
> Yet loss and gain become one whole.

Viorst again: 'The death of someone we love revives our childhood fears of abandonment, the ancient anguish of being little and left.'

This anguish I experienced terrifyingly when I was as old as about 12, when I became lost and separated from the family on Mont St Michel during a family holiday in Brittany. Lost and abandoned in a foreign land ... I now understand my depression of a month ago, and why the loss of Betty could so combine with the ageing losses to make a *double destitution*: I became 'little and lost again'. Even if I was a 'strong' partner with Betty, she, after all, was the architect of much of our living together, she was responsible for a lot of the daily arrangements; six or seven years ago it was she who nursed me through two months of flu and chest infection from which I might have died (according to my doctor son-in-law) had she not done so. So one of my losses in losing Betty is the loss of the most important adult in my life 'protecting' the child in me. Then the ageing losses have made me doubt my own competence, my own capacity to cope, my own ability to look after myself – so there has been the loss of the other adult looking after the child. No wonder these losses have stimulated anxiety, of which I have a high level in a generalised form anyway.

14 January 1995

Without ever having intended to, and having told no other soul, I told Helen about the incident of going to the Retirement Home for a meeting but encountering the bereaved warden and staying with her to give what comfort I could. She said 'it was meant'. I said that that is exactly what Betty would have said. She used to say that sort of thing rather frequently and, I thought, rather facilely, but in this case I believe it to be true; so why not in other cases? That sort of thing has certainly happened to me, sometimes, on other occasions, but never so strikingly as in that instance. Helen said it happened to her, as it undoubtedly happened to Betty, and she talked about being a 'channel'. Betty thought in terms of being a channel for Jesus, Helen did not see it like that but as a channel for 'Something', she knew not what. It was very much like that for me; and that something was essentially Good.

I was astonished when Helen told me that Betty had told her that, when she (Betty) was a small child, she was consciously aware of a need to comfort her mother. Paradoxically she connected this with the fact that her mother did not love her. Her mother used to say to her: 'You are not my child, you are Bertha's'. (Bertha was her nanny.)

Helen maintained that hormones and glandular secretions could affect one's physical state in severe bereavement – with an increased production of adrenalin stimulating other hormones, as in the 'fight or flight' reaction in fear. I wonder if she is right – I haven't come across the idea in my readings – although many do speak of the exacerbated sexual reaction, which is in the same sort of field. Could help to produce the depression too.

27 January 1995

Viorst is good on the loss of childhood innocence and the discovery of death.

'The essence of childhood consciousness is an illusion that we can live in a state of absolute safety. And living for ever and ever in a state of absolute safety is an irresistible, hard-to-relinquish illusion.'

'We finally learn in mid-life that no matter how well-behaved we are, we will die. We finally learn that there is no safety out there. We give up our childhood belief that if only we'll be good boys and girls, we'll be for ever protectively taken care of. Disaster and death, we discover fall on saint and sinner, on black hats and on white hats, alike. And while we may not choose to live out our lives as sinners and black hats, this discovery can free us to confront what Freud calls our id and what Gould describes as "our darker, mysterious center" – and to use some of the energies and passions that we find there to open up and revitalise our life.'

Is that a partial description of my mid-life crisis, which released some of the energies which opened up and revitalised my life, producing the astonishing output of the next twelve years?

Viorst gives perfect expression to the angry feelings I wrote down earlier at society's imposition of the 'dirty old man' stereotype. She writes: 'Sexually we are neutered by the silent message that lust in old age is unseemly, that the fires of passion should either burn out or be screened. Everyone knows – or should know – that not only "dirty" but "clean" old men and women can want and can have a sex life in their last decades. But the image of aging flesh enmeshed in lustful sexual acts remains, for many – most – people a repellent one.

In a sensitive study of age an eloquent Englishman, Ronald Blythe, describes how society unsexes the old, noting that "should an old person not seem to be in full repressive control of these urges, he or she is seen as either dangerous or pathetic, though nastily so in both instances. The old often live half lives, because they know that they would arouse disgust and fear if they attempted to live whole ones. All passion is not necessarily spent at seventy and eighty, but it pays the old to behave as if it were"'.

I still find myself frequently saying to Betty 'Oh darling' – in a sort of acceptance of the sadness. This continuing sadness is different from the earlier grinding, agonising, screaming pain of sheer grief, in which I just didn't know what to do with myself.

I think I can feel myself coming to the edges of something I could call peace. Where there is some peace, it is easier for joy to make its appearance. What is 'peace' in this sense? What is 'the peace of God which passes all understanding?' I've tried to analyse this. Is it not, really, simply a confidence that, *basically*, 'everything is all right'. That surely must mean 'Everything is all right with me' – because never is there a time when everything is all right with the world. In this bereavement situation, I suppose it also means a confidence that I know I can cope with the sorrow; sorrow will continue to be – but I have been through the worst of the storm.

I have earlier noted a number of similes and metaphors for the bereavement process. Another one has occurred to me. It is like a journey through a treacherous swamp where you have never been before; and those who help you most on this painful path are not those who take your arm and hold you up during your passage, and certainly not those who would, in their compassion and generosity, actually carry you across; for it is a journey which you can only make alone. Those who help you most are those who, although you realise they appreciate your predicament, do not show you exactly where to put your feet, but who enable you to see for yourself where you have to place them; and that there are no short cuts.

I do not like the word 'immortality' – except in the sense that the works of Shakespeare have achieved immortality. Immortality suggests a 'going on of the same', and I do not think of the going on through death in that way. I think of it as a going on to something larger.

10 February 1995

I find it very difficult to believe that it is sixteen months since Betty died – so time is still playing tricks. On the one hand this Big, Enormous Thing has still only just happened – and yet on the other, this last sixteen months has been unending. I have a better grasp of the days of the week now, although 'time of year' is still vague and elusive. For the last eighteen months the seasons and the festivals have largely passed me by; it has been a flat existence. The passage of time is not marked in the usual way.

I no longer feel the same compulsion to write in this diary; there is less to say – I suppose because there is less change, I don't think I have really wept for two or three months – although every day I am still frequently exclaiming 'Oh darling!' – which I suppose is an expression of remembrance and sadness, an acknowledgement to Betty of my continuing loss, which I think is something I shall always have for the rest of my life; but there is now an element of 'Heigh ho! Well, this is how it is, and here I am feeling it again.'

Although I have not wept for two or three months, there have been times when I wished I could. I suppose weeping serves to release inner emotional tension and pressure, and when you cannot obtain that release you feel as uncomfortable as you do when you have inner bodily pressures and yet are unable to get rid of the relevant secretions or excretions; the inability to weep gives you a sort of emotional constipation. Helen said that quiet tears might well up without the body-shaking sobbing of before; this was useful, and not to be denied, nor to be encouraged to develop into sobbing. In a sense, I had 'done the sobbing bit'. I can recognise that; it just leaves the sadness, without the pain that makes you want to scream.

2 March 1995

I have not really wept for three or four months now, but the tears do well up occasionally. Betty's birthday two days ago, when she would have been 77, affected me very little.

Now I can look back on the worst of my grief and say 'That was terrible! I think the most painful experience of my life.' Does not the fact that I can use the past tense about it suggest that I have entered another stage in the mourning process? That I am beginning 'to let my grief go?'

Pauline has lent me an interesting book by one Stanley Keleman *Living Your Dying*, which is quite good, although written in a rather difficult staccato style. The basic idea is that living and dying are processes which merge into each other and are each part of the other. Keleman quotes as follows (p.102): 'Norman O. Brown has said that only a person with unlived lives is afraid to die. A person who feels he has lived his life – the way he wanted – is not afraid. The fear of dying is tied to the goals of who you believe you have to be rather than who you are.' I can go along with that. I am so lucky to have been allowed to reach this point, where I don't feel I have unlived lives that I wish I had had.

9 March 1995

I notice that a month ago I remarked that I had not really wept for two or three months, and sometimes wished I could. Quite suddenly, this morning, I got my wish: there it was again, a great wave of pain sweeping over me, I knew the pain was always there really, one just had to live with it and get on with life. This time it broke through once again in a great weeping fit that did not subside very quickly, all the real shaking/sobbing, thigh-hitting, heel drumming, and shouting 'Oh darling, I MISS you so, I Miss you so – oh so much, so much', utterly spontaneously passionately, so I did not try to resist it. Triggered, of course by Madam Butterfly and Elgar's Nimrod Variation – corny, I know, to be affected like that by such 'popular classics', but there it is, that's how it was, even if not very sophisticated! I suppose in trying to make a new life and just get on with it, one pushes all the pain and loss below the surface, although one knows it is still there and at times one does not feel it so acutely all the time as it used to be a year ago, but then at intervals it has to break through. I suppose the business of 'letting one's grief go' means that the intervals get longer, but I was taken a bit by surprise.

28 March 1995

I have recently realised that, whereas in the darkness of the last eighteen months there were occasional arrows of joy, there were flashes of light penetrating the gloom, it was a matter of just carrying on doggedly through the murk, grateful for these intermittent illuminations but not expecting more. Looking back on this last eighteen months, I see it very much as a darkness, impenetrable for a long time, but in the last six months becoming more crepuscular. Now I think the light is growing, and perhaps for the first time I can acknowledge that I am beginning again to experience what can only be described as the joy of living.

Another recent realisation, quite distinct, is that in contemplating each day ahead, I do not have to spend much of it doing what someone else determines: I decide for myself what I am going to do, how I am going to spend my time. No employer dictates to me any more; even if the employment was of my own choosing, there were always many parts of what occupied me which were not. The relief of no longer being burdened by the editing of the Conference papers is only now beginning to sink in and 'settle' me, seven months after its publication; even if taking it on was originally my own voluntary choice, it turned into a six-year-long corvée which I had not anticipated.

In addition, in looking ahead at my day, I realise I no longer have Betty to consider, and her needs and wants. Having experienced this absence of Betty as the most grievous loss, initially I found this realisation shocking, and, to start with, unwanted. But if I am to be honest I have to acknowledge it to be so. After I retired and Betty's disabilities progressively worsened, I consciously accepted that my No 1 job for that stage of my existence was to look after her. What is more it became very rewarding, even if, understandably, Betty could not always accept my services graciously, and there were times of irritation – of anger, even – and of frustration and weariness. Now I do not have that self-chosen obligation. I am that much more able to choose for myself how I spend my time and energy every day.

This lack of constraints from other people amounts to a new-found freedom. A realisation of the particular one in relation to Betty brings a feeling of guilt – to put it in its most brutal wording – 'Betty's death has given you your freedom', which evokes a cry of 'No, no, it's not like that, I never *wanted* my freedom at that price'. What I have to realise is that this is yet one more paradox which holds contraries together and is nearer the truth than either by itself. The anguish at Betty's loss is true, the freedom is true. I have to embrace both.

30 August 1995

Two or three weeks of depression; waking up every morning with this great heaviness weighing down on me. Have the silly feeling that because it is nearly two years since Betty died, I 'ought not' to feel depressed like this. I suppose it is inevitable that I shall have bouts of it for a long time to come.

'Your grief is never finished.' I suppose I accepted that in an intellectual way, but thought that perhaps the physical manifestations of my grief would not break through any more – after all, I had not wept for Betty for four or five months. How wrong I could be. In the last twenty-four hours I have wept uncontrollably. The trigger? Something so obvious I should have been prepared for it. I kept all the letters Betty ever wrote me, and the time has come to see that if I should die tomorrow they are not a burden to my children, wondering what to do with them. Either I must destroy them all myself now, or I must bundle them up and mark them to be destroyed at my death. However, I found I could not do either without reading them through again. They were not in good order, so the first thing was to arrange them in a chronological fashion. Having done that, I started reading them through, in quite a matter-of-fact manner, it was just the next job which had to be done. It was all right at first, but by the time I had read through the first six months after we declared ourselves to each other and the correspondence had become passionate and voluminous, the tears were often flowing. I should have had the wit to know this would happen, but I had not anticipated it. When it did happen I made no attempt to restrain it.

It so happened that the day after I started doing this I was due to visit Helen, and it was natural to tell her what was happening. The result was I broke down completely. I made no apology, just let it happen. It was almost as if she expected it: 'You still have grieving to do' was all she said, and gave me the necessary quietness. I said I was not going to insult her by apologising. 'Why apologise for something as natural as weeping?' she said, 'You do not apologise for sneezing.'

After some time, I commented that in re-reading those letters, I had seen the importance of the period they represented, in a way I had not been completely aware of at the time, I was too busy living it. 'You now have the opportunity to experience the experience' she said. 'Yes!' I cried 'I am now old enough.' I tried to explain that I was not angry or sad, perhaps a bit nostalgic, and not resentful that I no longer had Betty, I was just so stirred up it was like pure emotion. I knew I could be happy for her joy. 'Her indescribable joy', echoed Helen, 'while you have grief. They are complementary, and need each other. Grief is the hardest lesson of all to learn' she said. 'Yes' I said, 'it's like nothing else, isn't it?'.' 'Do you feel Betty close to you?' she asked. 'Oh yes' I said. 'When you were weeping I could see her standing by you, stroking your hair, and then sitting on the floor at your feet, in a sort of glow.' 'Yes' I agreed, and surprised myself by saying 'and the glow was a sort of lightish blue.' 'Yes', said Helen, 'and blue is not a colour I usually see.'

CHAPTER 5

After Two Years

1 October 1995

Two years since Betty died. Time still playing funny tricks. In some ways that two years seems a great stretch of weary time; in other ways, it seems as if it was only yesterday that Betty died.

Your grief doubles back on you, wisely said Judith Viorst (p.278). How true that is: as we saw in the last entry when after four months of not weeping, I then spent four days doing little else. Now for the last three or four weeks, it is again following the pattern, of depression succeeding the tears. It is only when I wake up in the morning, when it is very heavy; but not too heavy to prevent me getting out of bed, which real complete depression can do, as I know. By the time I've had my breakfast it has considerably lifted, and I get on with the tasks of the day. It is not that I am dreading those tasks or do not want to face them; I am enjoying my life, and there are many things I can look forward to in the coming day with pleasurable anticipation. In the split second when I first wake and consciousness returns, there is a moment when the oblivion of sleep continues to blot out the grief. Then I suddenly become conscious of all the circumstances of my life, of which the biggest, buzzing, blooming fact is my loss of Betty and this hits me again with renewed freshness. It is like starting each day with a fresh losing of Betty. Is it at all surprising that this should be depressing? It helps to count my blessings, and to spend my usual time in meditation.

25 October 1995

I think I have at last achieved some peace but I cannot really claim to have achieved tranquillity. My reaction was: 'Well, what do you expect?' It's too soon to achieve tranquillity. When you have had such a great rock thrown into the pool of your existence, it takes a long, long time for the ripples to subside. The ripples may have become peaceful and no longer turbulent, but they are still there; it will be a long time before the water is perfectly tranquil. Of course I am impatient – but then we all are. 'It takes two years' say the experts. Now that the two year period is up, I tend to think the process should be completed and that I should have achieved tranquillity – but the process stretches out much longer than that. Virginia said: 'It's not surprising you still feel your grief after two years, sometimes intensely. *It is still a short time.*'

I think there will always be times when it is still a short time.

December 1995

As usual I went for my ten days art course in Derbyshire, which had always given me so much pleasure up until two years ago. That year it was only a couple of months after Betty had died, and I was just going through the motions in a mechanical sort of fashion. The following year I did not enjoy it, I was not enjoying life, and there was one occasion which made me very angry. So this year I wondered very much how it would be. Suddenly on the fourth day I realised *I was enjoying myself.* I had enjoyed every day. *I was enjoying life again.* What is more, I could allow myself to do so, without feeling guilty. I know that is what Betty would want.

July 1996

I think at last I am achieving some tranquillity. There are times when I still get stabbed with grief and nostalgia, and these reminding occasions can still sometimes call forth the tears, but they can now be accommodated in a greater serenity than among the turbulent emotions erupting two years ago. One such occasion was recently when I went to look at the wild roses where they grow in abundance, which I took Betty to see from the car for the last time three years ago. 'Oh darling!' still springs spontaneously from my lips, but these conversations with her are now more comfortable and less agonised.

September 1996

At some point in the above account I mentioned that the bereavement had taken away my self-confidence. I think that at last I have got it back again now. But it has taken three years.

I suppose I could be said to have done quite a lot in 'building a new life'. I still find it too pressured, with too many dead-lines. This has to be my own fault: I am still no better at saying 'No'. The hooks from my geological and academic life still drag at me, and the fact that I am still interested and cannot cut it off completely makes me vulnerable to requests to write things and do things, so I am often torn in two between inclination and disinclination. I have succeeded in writing the draft of a

1,000 page autobiography but this is largely a self-imposed task, and an enormous job of editing remains. I love my painting and drawing, but I still have to fight to find time to do it. I find it difficult to keep 'free days' in my diary. I suppose I have given a bit more time to Quaker things. I do manage to read the whole of *The Friend* every week, and I had the most wonderful spiritual 'boost' when I spent a fortnight at Woodbrooke last Easter. More heart fibrillation trouble, so that I cannot walk as much or as far as I used to, although I did manage to climb Pendle Hill. So I've taken to swimming every week. Music is a tremendous joy, as my darling children gave me a CD system for my 80th birthday, and that is magical.

April 1997

The other night I had a terrifyingly vivid dream. I was in a completely empty room, searching for something along the wainscoting. I had a clear picture of a small rectangular piece of wood in the wainscot, low down near the floor, different from the rest of the wainscot, but I could only half identify it; I pressed it to see if it concealed some sort of opening, but it would not move. Dominant in my mind the whole time was the fact that I had murdered Betty. This so filled me with horror and terror that it blanketed everything else. This was something that had happened and I knew it; it was insupportable. Then Betty II was standing there, young, attractive and vivacious, talking with me, and I knew I had married a second time. I knew she was Betty II, but the overwhelming terror was still in everything. Only gradually did I emerge into half-consciousness, and realise, with colossal relief, that what I had dreamed was only a sleeping fantasy, and not fact. Nevertheless, something of the terror remained for days.

Does this dream express the conflicting emotions I am still going through? At one and the same time wanting to 'let Betty go' and also to 'repossess' her? I know I have to let 'the old Betty' go – and yet there is a part of me that resists this and does not want to. I welcome 'the new Betty', with whom I have a relationship *now* and for whom I have provided a new psychic space, and yet there is some confusion. The rectangular piece of wood near the ground, which I tried to move but could not – could this symbolise Betty's coffin? A lingering, hopeless desire to recapture 'the old Betty?' Anyway, perhaps the dream has helped to bring into my con-sciousness the need to 'let the old Betty go', the need not to feel guilty about this; to know that this is not a disloyalty, but that the whole process of veering my thoughts to the current Betty is bound to be confusing.

May 1997

Nothing has been done to this diary for a long time because Helen had it to edit. However, she became ill and was unable to, so I have now got it back from her to try to round it off. For this purpose I have read the whole thing, and this has had the effect of reminding me that I am now in a very different state from that I was in three years ago. I can see that I have, in fact, travelled quite a long journey in my mourning over the last three-and-a-half years. Although the loss is always there, I have done a lot to 'let my grief go' and to 'repossess' Betty. I am calmer than I was; one might even say that sometimes I approach serenity. They say that grief is the price you have to pay for love – the greater the love the greater the grief. By that accounting, ours was a great love. I am happy to pay the price.

The gold flame of the wheat
May spring from a barren heart.
Love is not changed by Death
And nothing is lost
And all in the end is harvest.

Edith Sitwell

Who has left a scent on my life and left my walls
Dancing over and over with her shadows,
Whose hair is twined in all my waterfalls .....
        So I am glad
That life contains her with her moods and moments ....
        So that if now alone
I must pursue this life, it will not be only
A drag from numbered stone to numbered stone
But a ladder of angels, river turning tidal!

Louis Macniece

Quotations

I WAS OFFERED MANY 'comfortable words', in the form of poems, prayers and quotations. These can be useful in helping a bereaved person, but have to be chosen with great care to be suitable for that person, depending somewhat on the nature of their faith, or indeed, whether they have any; what is comforting to one is trite, facile, sentimental, mere wish-fulfilment or plain false to another. I received the following, in some cases on illuminated cards.

1. Christ is the Morning Star, who when the night of this world is past brings to His Saints the promise of the Light of Life and opens ever-lasting day.

Ven. Bede

2. God has created me to do Him some definite service; He has committed some work to me which he has not committed to another. I have my mission – I may never know it in this life, but I shall be told it in the next.

I am a link in a chain, a bond of connection between persons. He has not created me for naught. I shall do good, I shall do His work. I shall be an angel of peace, a preacher of truth in my own place *while not intending it* – if I do but keep His commandments.

Therefore I will trust Him. Whatever, wherever I am, I can never be thrown away. If I am in sickness, my sickness may serve Him; if in perplexity, my perplexity may serve Him; if I am in sorrow, my sorrow may serve Him. He does nothing in vain. He knows what he is about. He may take away my friends, He may throw me among strangers. He may make me feel desolate, make my spirits sink, hide my future from me – still He knows what He is about.

Cardinal Newman

3. A Prayer in Suffering

Dear Lord and Saviour, Jesus Christ, I hold up all my weakness
to your strength, my failure to your faithfulness, my sinfulness to your
perfection, my loneliness to your compassion, my little pains to your
great agony on the Cross.

I pray that you will cleanse me, strengthen me, guide me, so that
in all my ways my life may be lived as you would have it lived, without
cowardice, and for you alone. Show me how to live in true humility,
true contrition, and true love. Amen.

M.S.

4. Underneath are the everlasting arms.

Deuteronomy 33, 27

[It is ironical to read the whole verse from which this oft-quoted
extract comes; it is considerably more blood-thirsty, and reads: 'The
eternal God is thy refuge, and underneath are the everlasting arms:
and he shall thrust out the enemy from before thee: and shall say,
Destroy them.']

5. Fear not, for I have redeemed thee, I have called thee by thy name;
thou art mine. When thou passest through the waters, I will be with
thee; and through the rivers, they shall not overflow thee: when thou
walkest through the fire, thou shalt not be burned: neither shall the
flame kindle upon thee. For I am the Lord thy God, the Holy One
of Israel, thy Saviour.

Isaiah 43, 1-3

6. Footprints

One night I had a dream. I dreamed I was walking along the beach
with God and across the sky flashed scenes from my life. For each
scene I noticed two sets of footprints in the sand, one belonged to
me and the other to God.

When the last scene of my life flashed before us I looked back at
the footprints in the sand. I noticed that at times along the path of
life there was only one set of footprints. I also noticed that it
happened at the very lowest and saddest times of my life. This really
bothered me and I questioned God about it. "God, you said that once
I decided to follow you, you would walk with me all the way but I
noticed that during the most troublesome times in my life there is
only one set of footprints. I don't understand why in times when I
needed you most, you would leave me."

God replied, "My precious, precious child, I love you and would
never, never leave you during your times of trials and suffering. When
you see only one set of footprints it was then that I carried you."

Anon

7. Hearts being sick, minds nothing can.

E.E. Cummings

8.   Man was made for joy and woe;
And when this we rightly know
Safely through the world we go.
Joy and woe are woven fine,
A clothing for the soul divine;
Under every grief and pine
Runs a joy with silken twine.

William Blake

9. And death shall have no dominion.

Dylan Thomas

10. A ship sails and I stand watching till she fades on the horizon and someone at my side says, "she is gone". "Gone where?" Gone from my sight, that is all; she is just as large as when I saw her. The diminished size, and total loss of sight is in me, not in her, and just at the moment when someone at my side says "She is gone", there are others who are watching her coming, and other voices take up a glad shout, "There she comes!", and that is dying.

Bishop Brent

11. Death is nothing at all. I have only slipped away into the next room.

    I am I and you are you. Whatever we were to each other that we are still. Call me by my old familiar name, speak to me in the easy way you always used. Put no difference into your tone, wear no forced air of solemnity or sorrow. Laugh as we always laughed at the jokes we enjoyed together. Pray, smile, think of me, pray for me. Let my name be ever the household word that it always was. Let it be spoken without an effort, without the ghost of a shadow on it. Life means all that it ever meant. It is the same as it ever was, there is absolutely unbroken continuity.

    What is death but a negligible accident? I am waiting for you, for an interval, somewhere very near, just round the corner. All is well.

Canon Scott-Holland

[Someone sent this to Richard when they lost Mathew, and he found it very helpful.]

12. We seem to give them back to Thee, O God who gavest them to us.
Yet as thou didst not lose them in giving, so do we not lose them by
their return. Not as the world giveth, givest thou O Lover of souls.
What Thou givest Thou takest not away, for what is thine is ours also
if we are thine. And life is eternal and love is immortal, and death is
only an horizon, and an horizon is nothing save the limit of our sight.
Lift us up, strong Son of God that we may see further; cleanse our
eyes that we may see more clearly, draw us closer to Thyself that we
may know ourselves to be nearer to our loved ones who are with Thee.
And while Thou dost prepare a place for us, prepare us also for that
happy place, that where Thou art we may be also for evermore.

Bishop Brent

13. They that love beyond the World, cannot be separated by it.
    Death cannot kill what never dies,
    Nor can spirits ever be divided
    that love and live in the same Divine Principle,
    the Root and Record of their Friendship.
    If Absence be not Death, neither is theirs.

Death is but crossing the World, as Friends do the Seas;
    they live in one another still,
    For they must needs be present,
    that love and live in that which is Omnipresent.
    In this Divine Glass, they see Face to Face;
    and their converse is Free, as well as Pure.

William Penn (1693)

14.   Friends Departed

They are all gone into the world of light!
    And I alone sit lingering here;
Their very memory is fair and bright,
    And my sad thoughts doth clear.

It glows and glitters in my cloudy breast
    Like stars upon some gloomy grove,
Or those faint beams in which this hill is dressed,
    After the sun's remove.

I see them walking in an air of glory,
    Whose light doth trample on my days:
My days, which are at best but dull and hoary,
    Mere glimmering and decays.

O holy Hope! and high Humility,
    High as the heavens above!
These are your walks, and you have showed them me,
    To kindle my cold love.

Dear beauteous Death! the jewel of the Just,
    Shining nowhere but in the dark;
What mysteries do lie beyond thy dust,
    Could man outlook that mark!

He that hath found some fledg'd bird's nest may know,
    At first sight, if the bird be flown;
But what fair well or grove he sings in now,
    That is to him unknown.

And yet, as angels in some brighter dreams
    Call to the soul, when man doth sleep;
So some strange thoughts transcend our wonted themes,
    and into glory peep.

If a star were confined into a tomb
    Her captive flames must needs burn there;
But when the land that locked her up gives room,
    She'll shine through all the sphere.

O Father of eternal life, and all
    Created glories under thee!
Resume thy spirit from this world of thrall
    Into true liberty.

Either disperse these mists, which blot and fill
    My perspective still as they pass,
Or else remove me hence unto that hill,
    Where I shall need no glass.

Henry Vaughan (1621-1695)

15.   Do not stand at my grave and weep
             I am not there. I do not sleep.
             I am a thousand winds that blow
             I am the diamond glints on snow
             I am the sunlight on ripened grain
             I am the gentle autumn rain.
             When you awaken in the morning's hush,
             I am the swift uplifting rush
             Of quiet birds in circled flight.
             I am the soft stars that shine at night.
             Do not stand at my grave and cry,
             I am not there; I did not die.

Anon

[Written by a soldier in Northern Ireland, not long before he was killed by the I.R.A. Richard picked it up when he heard it broadcast on his car radio.]

16. I have just come across the following:

To grieve is also to celebrate the depth of the union. Tears are then the jewels of remembrance, sad but glistening with the beauty of the past. So grief in its bitterness marks the end ... but it is also praise to the one who is gone.

James A. Peterson
On Being Alone: a guide for widowed persons

17. Nothing that comes to you is negative. I mean *nothing* ... All the trials and tribulations, and the biggest losses you ever experience ... are gifts to you. It is an opportunity that you are given to grow. You will not grow if you sit in a beautiful flower garden and someone brings you gorgeous food on a silver platter. But you will grow if you are sick, if you are in pain, if you experience losses, and if you do not put your head in the sand, but take the pain and learn to accept it, not as a curse or a punishment, but as a gift to you, with a very, very specific purpose.

Elizabeth Kübler-Ross

APPENDIX II

Books

I HAVE MADE NO attempt to survey the literature available on the subject of bereavement, but it might be useful to mention the books which I personally have come across and found useful.

The best were:
Tatelbaum, Judy. *The Courage to Grieve.*
Viorst, Judith. *Necessary Losses.*

The next best were:
Jones, Mary. *Secret Flowers.* Women's Press Ltd.
Truman, Jill. *Letter to my Husband.* Hodder & Stoughton.

Also useful were:
Lehmann, Rosamond. *The Swan in the Evening.*
Stott, Mary. *Forgetting's No Excuse.*

The following is a quite excellent anthology, which can lead on to other things:
Whittaker, Agnes. *All in the end is Harvest.* Darton, Longman & Todd.

Of course Elizabeth Kübler-Ross's book *Death: the final stage of growth* is quite excellent, although it is more about the handling of death than strictly about bereavement as such. Colin Murray Parkes's book *Bereavement* is good, and exhaustive, but it is clinical in its approach, and is more for the supporters and counsellors of the bereaved than for the bereaved themselves.

C.S. Lewis's *A Grief Observed* I read first some forty years ago in a somewhat academic fashion and had little memory of its contents, so I read it again. This time, out of my own experience, I found it disappointing; it did not speak to my condition at all, and there is some very questionable psychology in it.

APPENDIX III

Hints on Comforting

A S A RESULT OF MY experience in losing Betty, I would give the following advice to anyone who wants to comfort or express sympathy towards a bereaved person:

1. What most bereaved persons want most of all is an *acknowledgement* of their pain. If you see them, don't suppose that your sympathy can be taken for granted; say *something*. Do not be put off by the knowledge that 'Everyone can master a grief but he that has it' (Shakespeare). People are often shy about saying anything, because they are sensitive to the bereaved person's grief; they fear they may be 'intruding', and they are mindful of Goldsmith's words 'Premature consolation is but the remembrancer of sorrow'; they feel (rightly in one sense) that no mere words can 'make it better', and they don't know what to say. So, say *something*, however stumbling. There is, after all, quite a choice of what to say, from a simple 'I'm so sorry' through 'My thoughts and prayers are very much with you' to a direct 'I love you'. The 'saying' is much helped if it can be accompanied by a little body language – from a hand-on-the-shoulder or a warm hand-clasp to a cheek-kiss or an enveloping hug – according to how well you know the person and how comfortable you are with the body language. If you have already written to the person when you first see them after their bereavement, do not suppose that this lets you out of some current expression – maybe just a silent hug. If the encounter brings tears to the bereaved person, don't tell them not to cry; say rather: 'Let the tears flow, they are an expression of your love.'

2. Write: as soon as possible. Don't be inhibited by the difficulty of writing this sort of letter, nor by the feeling that a mere letter cannot heal the bereaved person's wound. Do not feel that it is now too late if you hear of the death some months afterwards; it is never too late. Use your own spontaneous wording to:

i) express your sympathy for the bereaved person;

ii) say all the appreciative things about the dead person you can, even if it has to be a bit conjectural in cases where you knew them only a little or not at all. This part is sometimes the most comforting aspect of your letter for the bereaved person. Some writers of letters of 'condolence' (dreadful word!) leave this bit out altogether, but it is most important.

iii) you may have a poem or quotation, or a religious affirmation of faith, whose appropriateness for the particular bereaved person you have to judge, whether to use it or not. What may be comforting words to one may seem to be facile wishful thinking to another. [For a selection of these, see Appendix I.]

iv) Repeat the sympathy in a slightly different form, extending it from the immediate present to the coming months, making the person realise that you know it is a pain which will continue for a very long time.

3. Be prepared at any time to *listen* to the bereaved person, give them an opportunity to talk about the dead person, to tell the story of their last months, to recount how they died, and, if the bereaved person shows signs of wanting to do so, about their own reactions and feelings. This is usually very important in helping the bereaved person to accept the reality of the death and come to terms with their loss. Don't make the mistake of thinking that it is the unmentionable subject, that you mustn't 'reopen the wound'.

4. At funerals, memorial services, inscriptions on cards with flowers and suchlike, be positive. Joy and thankfulness for the dead person's life can balance sympathy for the grievous loss of the bereaved. The balance is crucial; joy can shine through the tears, but both are real. The parson conducting Elizabeth Munnings's funeral overdid the joy bit, and told the mourners that tears were wrong; it was he who got the balance wrong.

5. It may be appropriate in some cases to suggest a book to read. [A few possibilities are listed in Appendix II.]